The Dissemination of Music

MUSICOLOGY: A BOOK SERIES
Edited by Hans Lenneberg, The University of Chicago, Illinois

This book is part of a series. The publisher will accept continuation orders which may be cancelled at any time and which provide for automatic billing and shipping of each title in the series upon publication. Please write for details.

The Dissemination of Music

Studies in the History of
Music Publishing

Edited by

Hans Lenneberg

The University of Chicago
Illinois

Routledge
Taylor & Francis Group

LONDON AND NEW YORK

First published 1994 by
Gordon and Breach Science Publishers

Published 2013 by Routledge
2 Park Square, Milton Park, Abingdon, Oxfordshire OX14 4RN
711 Third Avenue, New York, NY, 10017, USA

First issued in paperback 2016

Routledge is an imprint of the Taylor & Francis Group, an informa business

---

British Library Cataloguing in Publication Data

Dissemination of Music: Studies in the
History of Music Publishing. —
(Musicology: A Book Series, ISSN 0275–5866;
Vol. 14)
   I. Lenneberg , Hans   II. Series
   070.579409

ISBN 13: 978-1-138-96779-3 (pbk)
ISBN 13: 978-2-88449-117-4 (hbk)

CONTENTS

INTRODUCTION TO THE SERIES

The Gordon and Breach Musicology series, a companion to the *Journal of Musicological Research*, covers a creative range of musical topics, from historical and theoretical subjects to social and philosophical studies. Volumes thus far published show the extent of this broad spectrum, from *Music, Film, and Art; Witnesses and Scholars: Studies in Musical Biography;* to *Music in English Children's Drama of the Later Renaissance.* The editors also welcome interdisciplinary studies, ethnomusicological works and performance analyses. With this series, it is our aim to expand the field and definition of musical exploration and research.

INTRODUCTION

Considering that there is hardly a publication these days that does not dismiss historical musicology as something either hopelessly passé, or at least in bad straits, it may seem daring to issue any book that openly shows its positivist face. This collection of essays focusing on the dissemination of music, the history of publishing, is historico-philological with a vengeance; but even though it may be out of fashion, to those who know that the overall picture of the musical past is not yet complete, each of the following essays makes an important contribution.

When Kerman in his book *Contemplating Music* opened a Pandora's box of criticism, citing Curt Sachs who urged us to see the big picture as long as forty years ago, he gave us a paragraph from one of the wisest scholars in our field I have ever known:

> Do not say wait! We are not yet ready; we have not yet dug up sufficient details to venture on such daring generalities. This argument . . . will still be heard a hundred years from now, at a time specialized research has filled and overflowed our libraries.
> . . . (Sachs in 1949 quoted by Kerman, *Contemplating Music*. Cambridge: Harvard University Press, p. 177)

Kerman is right of course to endorse Sachs. But the big boys, (pace feminist critics), such historians as Abert, Bukofzer, Lang, Sachs himself, always did see the big picture (in their days a lot easier, of course); still they went on with their piddling little studies such as e.g, "Ein neuer musikalischer Papyrus-Fund" (Abert), or studies of fauxbourdon (Besseler), the *Caput* mass (Bukofzer), and others, all of which contributed to the big picture for coming generations. New discoveries of however varying degrees of importance are still made. They change our critical perceptions and Kerman is wrong to relegate "positivist" research to those of our graduates not talented enough to be critics. Heaven help us with the scholars who have no special critical talent but now feel obliged to try their hands at it anyway. The late Howard Mayer Brown, arguably the best musicologist of his generation, a positivist if there ever was one, never wrote a book or article that did not contribute to the overall larger picture, yet he is hardly mentioned in *Contemplating Music*.

When it comes to a collection of essays such as this one, hypersophisticates may question the need for them. But as recently as ten years ago the term "dissemination of music" was hardly known and certainly not used. One spoke of the "music trade" with some disdain (since it was neither an art nor a learned discipline), and the literature about music publishing was largely about techniques of typesetting and printing. These subjects are still fundamental in the field if only for the need to establish hierarchies of sources for their dates and reliability. Once music printing began, several decades later than books, i.e., sometime around 1475, because of such difficulties as lining up staves and notes as well as text, it was formidable and expensive. Consequently there was probably a certain reluctance on the part of printer/publishers (at the time usually the same individual) to invest in the process and, as one might expect, the first published music consisted almost entirely of liturgical music for the Catholic services. Nevertheless, a surprising amount of publishing began almost immediately. One of the contributors to this book, Mary Kay Duggan, is an expert in this field. Her contribution on incunabula opens the volume with interesting news about early missals.

Naturally the moment one addresses such an issue as for whom and why publishers produced their work, one is really dealing with the social history of music. Thus even without displacing the history of printing, still essential to source studies, we have added a new topic of equal or potentially far greater importance, a topic about which still not very much is known. Since the archives of this kind of material are exclusively available in Europe, if anywhere, and are not obviously organized by subject (much of what would have been documentation printers may have suppressed because they took it to be trade secret), research has been rather slow. Some of what we have learned derives from digging in these archives but even more, I suspect, is encountered accidentally in the course of other unrelated research. Each of the specialized essays in this collection moves us forward bit by bit. Thus, for example, while hardly anything was known about Renaissance editors (were there even such creatures who made their living or part of it by working in publishing?), Dr. Ongaro's essay about a professional editor of anthologies represents a major step forward into the actual situation of publishing in the sixteenth century.

Professor Mangsen's essay, profusely documented with statistical tables, is directly related to the overall situation of publishing in Europe and indirectly to the history of changing taste. Why was Corelli so popular in England long after his death, while in Germany he is hardly mentioned at the same time?

Sarah Adams is interested in the international distribution of music in the late eighteenth century, a question that as far as I am concerned is still puzzling. Considering that music was inherently international, and in the absence of firmly established copyright laws, why was there not more piracy? There are some scholars who believe that the term "piracy" is misapplied in the eighteenth century — that the concept of intellectual property was only just surfacing and there was no ethical inhibition about appropriating music. But even if property rights were lodged in the publisher, Haydn and Mozart were quite anxious to protect themselves if only to sell their wares in other countries and in different arrangements. Both deplored the free taking of their works as theft. Adams presents us with a new perspective on the international music trade.

Bianca Maria Antolini has long been at work piecing together the history of music publishing in Italy. This contribution of hers illustrates not only how most Italian publishers began their careers as operatic copyists, but also the extent to which they hoped subscriptions would assure them of sales in what must have been a very uncertain business at the time.

Finally, listing the contributions in chronological order, Lisa Feurzeig illustrates what became a new relationship between publisher and composer in the course of the nineteenth century, when authors were now clearly the owners of their intellectual property. The changed relationship was never unequivocally beneficial to the composer and even today it is usually still a battle between profit and art. For the most part, what we know of this kind of business arrangement, beginning with Haydn and Beethoven, is very one-sided: the composer complains, but the publisher's correspondence has rarely been preserved. We can learn quite a bit from Fauré's unhappy "marriages" with publishers.

Aside from its inherent interest in the history of publishing and *Rezeptionsgeschichte*, I hope this collection will encourage similar work. We need not all work in semiology, gender studies, deconstructionism, and whatever other new trends will be around tomorrow. What we do need is to continue the necessary empirical scudwork not by default, for lack of talent, but rather because without it musicology will simply be rehashing what we already know in increasingly desperate guises.

Music in the Fifteenth-Century Printed Missal

MARY KAY DUGGAN

The introduction of hundreds of exactly replicated copies of the missal, the liturgical book of texts and chant for the celebrant of the Catholic Mass, affected the very nature of the service book and the plain chant it contained. The move to print the liturgy was accompanied by a complex web of technological, liturgical and political challenges that provoked reaction by printers and publishers, local and regional monastic and diocesan editors, and the very top echelons of monastic orders, ecclesiastical provinces, and the papacy. Missals form a large percentage of the corpus of early printed music put into the hands of fifteenth-century readers. Apparently well aware of the significance of the appearance of liturgical books in print, contemporary liturgical reform movements were intensely involved in the process of editorial revision and the production of corrected copy texts for the printers. The books themselves illustrate the manner in which printers responded to the challenges of transferring newly reformed manuscripts into print, through the design of layout, regional styles of chant, size relationship of music type to letter type in the absence of ruling, musica ficta, color for staves, complex melismatic neumes, liquescence, and mensural chant. From the first decades the publication of liturgical music displayed the characteristics of centralized and specialized production together with widespread distribution networks that were to contribute to the standardization of liturgical books and culminate after the Council of Trent in the next century in a monopoly by a single publisher appointed by Rome.

Music incunabula are usually defined as those books printed before 1501 containing music in the form of printed notes and staves, printed notes or staves, or printed text with space allocated by the printer for the addition of notes and staves by hand.[1] Current estimates suggest that some four hundred and fifty editions of a total of about 30,000 incunabula satisfy that definition of music incunabula; about 270 contain printed notes and staves.[2] Detailed study of 156 Italian music incunabula shows that most were printed with notes and staves from metal type, though in the earliest period of printing before such type was available a significant number were printed with space for music: 76 contain notes and staves printed from metal, 13 contain notes and staves printed from wood, 17

Table 1 A comparison of all music incunabula and Italian production.

Music Incunabula	Notes/ staves metal	Notes/ staves wood	TOTAL Notes/ staves	Stave	Space	Unverified	TOTAL
All	*	*	270	*	*	*	450
Italian	76	13	89	17	34	14	156
Italian Missals	61	2	63	13	28	14	118

* = research incomplete

contain printed staves, 34 have space allocated for music, and fourteen are titles for which no copy could be located or examined (see Table 1). Of 156 Italian music incunabula, 75% or 118 are missals;[3] an additional five missals[4] printed in Italy contain no music or space for music, though some owners inserted manuscript music on extra leaves bound in. A higher number of editions of the missal, 191, were printed in what incunabulists call German-speaking lands (the area covered today by Germany, Austria, Switzerland and parts of Eastern Europe).[5] Estimating that each of the Italian and German editions was issued in five hundred copies (the number of copies ordered, for examples by Abbot Udalricus III of the Benedictine Monastery of Michelsberg in Bamberg of the 1481 *Missale benedictinum* (Bamberg: Johann Sensenschmidt; H 1127), the combined total would be over 150,000 books, all but 10,000 printed between 1480 and 1500.

A missal is made up of a central portion of fixed prayers, the Canon, preceded by the readings for Sundays (Temporale) to Easter and followed by the Sundays after Easter and the readings for feast days (Sanctorale). The text of sung portions is written in smaller letters than those read by the priest or celebrant. Music notation is included for those portions sung by the celebrant, including a number of prefaces that vary according to the time of year and level of feast, the Pater noster, incipits of the chants of the Ordinary or unvarying parts of the service (Kyrie, Gloria, Credo, Sanctus, Agnus Dei), and a few chants for Holy Week. The choir's sung portion is contained in another liturgical book, the gradual. A calendar of feasts for the year, graded according to level of feast, is usually placed at the beginning of the missal. Unusual in the manuscript missal, preliminary material after the calendar grew in the printed missal to contain such extras as a letter from the bishop requesting those under him to purchase the book, explanation of the perpetual calendar, cautions to the priest in handling the host, prayers to be said while vesting, tables, and indexes. Titles of sections and readings, directions for the additions of sung portions (introit, psalm, antiphon, verse), and directions for actions of the priests appear in red, thus called rubrics.

Editions of fifteenth-century missals reflect prescriptions of various rites, the Roman rite being most common but others distinctive to localities (as, for example, Ambrosian to Milan, Sarum to England). One of the preoccupations of the Catholic Church councils in Constance and Basel in the first half of the fifteenth century had been monastic reform, including the development of a standard observance that could be accepted on both sides of the Alps. Benedictines at Melk in Austria, Subiaco in the Papal States, Padua in the Venetian Republic, and Bursfeld and Mainz in Germany played a major role in arguing for and developing a reformed liturgy.[6] Despite conflict between conciliar and papal authority which led the Council of Basel to elect a second pope in 1441, northern reform efforts continued. In 1448 at Mainz papal legate Cardinal Juan de Carvajal, an appointee of newly elected Pope Nicolas V who promised to unite Europe again under one pope, approved the new *Ordinarius divinorum* of the growing Bursfeld Congregation of Benedictines and specifically mentioned for the first time the need for standardized liturgical chant melodies as well as texts.[7] With Carvajal's papal entourage in Mainz was the German Nicolas of Cusa, former Basel conciliarist and soon to be made a cardinal and papal legate himself. In the capacity of papal representative he returned to Mainz in 1451 to decide against the reformed liturgical books prepared by the Benedictine house of St. James in Mainz and, with authorization to have recourse to secular arms if need be,[8] he pronounced in favor of the version prepared by the Bursfeld Congregation. The *Ordinarius divinorum* has been described as "really only an adaptation of the office of the Roman Curia for monastic use."[9] After joining the Bursfeld Congregation the Benedictines of St. James managed to issue their Psalter in 1459 and a *Canon missae* appeared in Mainz in 1458 (GW 5983), but the first printed missal was delayed until about 1472 when a *Missale romanum* (Goff M-643) appeared somewhere in Central Italy with an incipit attributing the editing to Franciscans, the order of the current pope Sixtus IV. Another undated missal appeared in equally obscure circumstances about 1473, a *Missale speciale* for the diocese of Constance. An alphabetic type similar to that of the first missal was used in Rome by Ulrich Han to print the 1475 *Missale romanum* (H 11364), reprinted with music in 1476 (H 11366) and often afterward by Han and his successor, both semi-official printers of papal documents. The Bursfeld Benedictines continued to negotiate as

Table 2 Missals Printed in the Fifteenth-Century in Italy and in German-speaking Lands.

Country	Roman Rite	Religious Order	Local Rite	Total
Italy	84	14	25	123
German-speaking	10	14	168	191

late as 1471 to print their liturgical books in Subiaco;[10] the *Ceremoniale* and *Ordinarius* appeared in 1474–75 from the press of the Brothers of the Common Life in Marienthal (HC 12059, Goff O–85; H 4883=12059, Goff S–756) and the missal in 1481 (H 11267) printed in Bamberg by Johann Sensenschmidt with the votive Masses and sequences integral to northern liturgical tradition.[11]

A comparison of missals produced in Italy with those printed in German-speaking lands (see Table 2) reveals a scarcity of editions in the Roman rite printed in Germany; if figures were available, that scarcity would be seen to hold true for the rest of Europe. North of the Alps, missals used outside the monastery were under the editorial control of the diocese although cathedral chapters were being urged in visitations by papal legates to bring local books into closer agreement with the practices of Rome. Widespread dissemination of printed Roman missals provided editors with easy access to those practices. Proof that printed missals became the exemplars for future editions is found in a copy of the *Missale romanun* (Venice: G. B. Sessa, 1497, H 11412*) that contains annotations in the hand of Cardinal Sirleto that were used for the reforms that produced the Tridentine missal under Pope Pius V after the Council of Trent in 1570.[12] The calendar and services of the Roman rite and the design and types of Italian printers as established in the tens of thousands of missals issued in the fifteenth century had a lasting impact.

Decisions on how and where to include music in printed books would have been made by an editor or editorial committee[13] and set down in a manuscript exemplar to serve as a copy text for the printer, but unfortunately no such copy text has been identified and the printed books must speak for the publication process. What is apparently the first printed missal, attributed to Central Italy about 1472, leaves so much space for insertions by hand of rubrics, music, and illuminations that both copies have at times been treated as manuscripts.[14] A copy was found in 1964 in the manuscript collections of the Biblioteca Vaticana (Urb. lat. 109, called BV below) in the intact library of Federico da Montefeltro, the Duke of

Urbino, for whom it was illuminated.[15] I recently identified another copy from a Central Italian Benedictine monastery, now in the Newberry Library (Inc. f7428.5, called NL below), also called a manuscript in the inventory made at the time of its purchase in 1890. The size of the book is Median folio (NL, 328 × 220mm heavily trimmed; BV, 348 × 243mm, slightly trimmed). Both copies are vellum rather than paper, since skin was traditionally preferred for manuscript liturgical books because of their heavy use and presumed longevity. Pages are laid out in two columns of twenty-nine lines of text or space for seven texted music staves. The edition first appeared (NL) with about one-third of the total space blank for text in red, music and initials to be added by hand. At some point it was decided to run the sheets through the press again to print in red rubrics of three or more lines (BV), still relying on a rubricator for isolated abbreviations for verses and responses. Space for Roman plainchant, for which type was still four years in the future, was left immediately following rubrics for performance on forty-seven of 692 pages, primarily for prefaces but also for such individual chants as the "Ecce lignum" of Good Friday and "Pater noster" of the Canon. That space was filled in by hand in both copies with plainchant in square Roman notation on two-, three-, and four-line red staves (see Fig. 1).

The relationship of music to alphabetic text in liturgical books had been carefully worked out in manuscripts and delineated in the ruling of pages that preceded scribal entry.[16] Whereas in the rest of the first missal the printer has allotted the space of three lines of text to each staff and to text underlay, this first appearance of music in the book is one line short and the solution was to leave both text and chant to be entered in manuscript. Presumably the sequence of scribal activity was black text, red lines for staves, black neumes, and red initials. Without the rules that were the usual guide for scribes, the space was approached quite differently in each copy. BV's music scribe chose to enter a two-line staff over the first line of text, allowing room for the first low note but placing the clef at the level of the line of text above. NL's music scribe placed the first low note in the text line, allowing room for three staff lines; the initial is designed for a larger space than is available here and intrudes over the clef of the second line. It is clear that the first "music" books that were printed with blank space for music to be entered by the owner vary enormously from copy to copy and required a great deal of effort to complete after purchase. In a large percentage of extant copies of incunable missals printed with space for music, no music was ever entered.

A printer who receives a text with passages of music can decide to omit them, leave space, print staff lines, or print lines and notes. While there are

(a)

(b)

Figure 1 The first appearance of music (f. [i5]ᵛ) in the ca. 1472 *Missale romanum*, (a) NL and (b) BV.

no extant printers' copy texts for missals, contemporary manuscript missals assure us that music for the celebrant was a regular feature of the genre. A printer's decision to leave space for music in a printed text acknowledges its importance to the reader and presumes the ability of owners to write in the passages for themselves, while also showing that the printer probably did not have access to music type. Printed staff lines perform the same functions with the additional benefits of providing a visual reminder to the reader that music belongs in the space, defining by the distance between staff lines the size of the notation, and providing the red color appropriate to staves for chant. The printer of a book with printed staves and without printed notes again probably did not have access to music type.

Another reason for the omission of printed notation, even by printers who were skilled in the use of music type, is the variety of regional styles of plainchant in use at the time. Books printed in Italy in the fifteenth century were distributed internationally from such cities as Venice, with its succcessful land and sea distribution network that made it the center of printing in the later decades of the century. While square Roman notation with a stemmed virga would be acceptable anywhere in Italy, German-speaking lands would expect *Hufnagelschrift* or horseshoe-nail notation, Milan used Ambrosian notation, medieval Hungary used a gothicized Roman called Messine-German, and Spain preferred an unstemmed virga.[17] Extant copies of editions of a given Roman missal with blank space for music or with printed staves without notes can be found with many different styles of music notation. Since Messine-German notation was never cut into type, the *Missale strigoniense* (for Eszterom or Gran) was printed several times with staves and without notes by a printer (Johann Emerich of Speier) who regularly printed Roman chant type in other books. Extant copies of such missals include manuscript notation in Messine-German, Gothic, and Roman styles.

The participation of international religious orders in editorial reform and the wide dissemination of Italian editions of liturgical books helped to erode regional styles of chant. When all liturgical books at the Benedictine monastery at Benediktbeuern were burned in a fire in 1490 and had to be replaced, the abbot complained that the choir books sent as exemplars from the Benedictine house at Tegernsee were in "modern" notation and his house preferred the "old" notation.[18] The Benedictines of Tegernsee were at the center of the liturgical reform movement coordinated with Subiaco and Padua. A manuscript missal from their library (Staatsbibliothek, Munich, Clm 19234) contains text in the southern gothic rotunda letter, Roman plain chant notation, rubrics, and design closely resembling the first printed missal, though at the end of the fifteenth century a calendar and Canon in northern gothic textura bookhand were inserted.

Beyond music notation styles, there were other significant differences in design between a northern and Italian missal. The first edition of the Benedictine missal (*Missale benedictinum bursfeldense*, Bamberg: Sensenschmidt, 1481) was commissioned by Abbot Ulrich III of Michelsberg in

Bamberg to be printed in 500 copies on vellum and paper. The size was slightly larger (Union Theological Seminary, New York, 365 × 259mm) than the usual Median folio, and some northern diocesan missals were printed on even larger Royal folio paper (*Missale wratislaviense*, Mainz: Peter Schoeffer, 1493, H 11333; Univerzitní knihovna, Prague, 40 A 8, 410 × 287mm). The letters of the Benedictine missal are in a gothic textura type (32 lines per page) and the music (9 staves per page) uniformily written in the dozen copies examined in a gothic plainchant notation remarkably like that later cut into type for Sensenschmidt's missals. The organization of the book differs in that the entire Temporale appears before the Canon which is followed by votive Masses, readings for particular feasts, and sequences. A major visual difference is the design of the central portion of the book, two gatherings of plainchant and the Canon, in a single column across the page, the Canon in a very large text type (12 lines per page in the Benedictine missal) and the chant on a large music staff (18mm, 9 lines a page). Music in northern missals was brought together in the gathering or gatherings preceding the Canon in a single-column format, rather than dispersed immediately following rubrics for use in a two-column layout.

The design of staves also varied from region to region in ways that would soon be lost as impossible or impractical via the technology of printing. Staves were uniformly red in the Italian Roman missal of the late fifteenth century and in manuscript form varied in number of lines from two to five as needed for the ambitus of the melody. Such variety in staff size is unusual in printed books, though a good music compositor following a manuscript model could accommodate it, as in the first missal with printed music (*Missale romanum*, Rome: Han, 1476) with four- and five-line staves. Reprints by Han's successor, Stephan Planck, changed to consistent five-line staves that made it easier for the printer to lay out notation. Erhard Ratdolt's first missal, the *Missale strigoniense* (Venice, 1486) includes staves of three, four, and five lines. The first music printed in German-speaking lands, the *Graduale* for the diocese of Constance ([Southern Germany? ca. 1473]; GW 5315), was printed on five-line black staves framed at each side by two rules forming a marginal space into which clefs and directs (*custos*) were inserted. In the unique extant copy (British Library, London, IB. 15154) the line of the F clef is visually accented by handcoloring in red. The importance in the north of a red line for "F" is attested to by the hand-drawn insertion of a single-line red staff for the handwritten gothic plainchant in the lower margins of the 1493 *Missale speciale* printed without music (Strasbourg, Grüninger; British Library, London, IB. 14180). In another northern missal (*Missale romanum*, Nuremberg: Fratres Ordinis Eremitarum S. Augustini, 1491; H 11262) three-line red staves appear for the three pages of chant. Pierre Attaignant cut the first single-impression plainchant type perhaps even earlier than his mensural type of 1529, but no printed sheets that use it survive, presumably because as long as red staves were demanded for plainchant a double impression was required.[19] Technological efficiency would eventually eliminate red for plainchant staves and standardize the number of staff lines for chant to four, resorting to ledger lines for a fifth if necessary.

One further notational possibility exists, that of supplying notation without staves. With painstaking care, neumes for chanting all epistles and gospels have been entered above the text in red *in campo aperto* in at least four copies of the *Missale benedictinum bursfeldense* (British Library, London, IB.2616; J. Pierpont Morgan Library, New York, ChL ff156; Bibliothèque Nationale, Paris, Vélins 245; Preussische Kulturbesitz, Berlin, Inc. 333, 2°). Even more frequent in incunable missals are handwritten neumes *in campo aperto* above the text of the gospels for Passion Sunday. Such tiny interlinear neumes are a technical impossibility in locked formes of metal type.

Early printed editions of the missal for the Ambrosian rite included space for music that was filled in one copy by two-line staves, one red line for "F" and one yellow line for "C" (*Missale ambrosianum*, Milan: Zarotto, 1475, H 11254; Biblioteca Ambrosiana, SP.II.22) and in another by raster-drawn red staves upon which the red line for "F" was strengthened and a yellow line for "C" drawn (Bibliothèque Nationale, Paris, Rès. B. 1485).[20] Later editions of the work (Milan: Valdarfer, 1482; Milan: Zarotto, 1488) included printed 4-line red staves. No printed missal included special colors to mark the location of clefs.

Type for music must abide by the tyranny of the rectangular forme into which pages are locked for printing and the rectangular metal shape of individual characters that must fit tightly side by side in that forme. On the other hand, beginning in the fifteenth century music type differed from alphabetic type in that it was not designed to be set in rows of pieces of type equal in height, but in a composite row equal in size to the staff. Individual music types of a single font are produced from more than one mold to accommodate designs of different heights such as tall (clefs, neumes of large intervals), medium (stemmed notes, neumes of small intervals), and small (accidentals, lozenges, liquescent neumes). Each piece of type could be set to print in black on a line or space of the staff already printed in red. As the compositor set designs for music notation, each piece of type had to be surrounded by spacing material so that type with faces and blank type would fit together like brickwork.[21] Thirty-eight music types were used in Italian music incunabula, thirty-three Roman plainchant (two of which included designs for printing the black mensural notation of the "Credo cardinalis" in the gradual), three Ambrosian plainchant, one gothic plainchant, and one white mensural notation.[22] All but five were used for missals, fifteen for folio format (staff of 15 to 21mm), nine for quarto format (staff of 10 to 14mm), and five for octavo format (staff of 9 to 11 mm). A table of the clefs of Italian music types in actual size illustrates the enormous range from very large choirbook format (staff of 32 to 55 mm) to small octavo.[23]

The rectangular shape of a piece of type encourages compactness of design through short stems on noteheads rather than a variety of stem lengths according to the height of a note on the staff, narrow directs at the end of a line for less of a visual cue for the placement of the note on the next line, and the elimination of pen strokes that had decorated clefs and neumes in manuscripts. That technological imperative may be responsible for the shape of the common note of printed plainchant, today

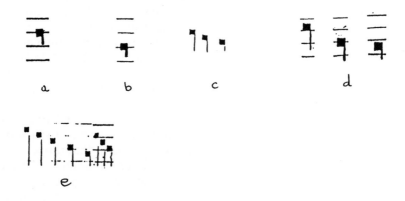

Figure 2 Stems of plainchant type.

   (a) Emerich of Speier, R19.
   (b) Torresani, R22.
   (c) Torresani, R23.
   (d) Ragazzoni, R14.
   (e) Valdarfer, R26.

familiar in the liturgical books printed by Desclée. Most plainchant missal type used one casting of the virga, with a short stem (Johann Emerich, 6mm, R19; Torresani, 5.5mm, R22, see Fig. 2a–b) while others included virgas of varying stem lengths designed to extend to the bottom of the staff from noteheads on various lines and spaces (Torresani, 6.75–12mm, R23; Ragazzoni, 6.5–11mm, R14; see Fig. 2c–d). An eclectic solution to the need for different stem lengths was chosen by Christoph Valdarfer, who apparently cast only the notehead and used pieces of metal rule cut to size for stems (R26, Fig. 2e). Difficulty in attaching the rules to the noteheads combined with the irregularity of weak rules makes the music a challenge to read.[24] Valdarfer was one of the few to successfully preserve variant lengths for the direct placed on different lines or spaces (R26).

In contrast to chant, mensural music has always been disseminated in an internationally recognized notation that could be read throughout Europe, and that notation has always included long note stems capable of extending through a five-line staff. The first such type appeared in Niger's *Grammatica* (Venice: Theodor Franck of Würzburg, 1480; M1) with designs for varying lengths of stems (6.5–13mm) and the well-known type of Petrucci appeared in 1501 with a long stem of a single size that often projected into the text above and below the staff. After Petrucci left the Republic of Venice to return to Fossombrone in the Papal States, where in 1513 he received a privilege to print music, a Venetian typefounder requested a fifteen-year privilege to protect the printing and sale of mensural music books in the Republic of Venice.

> ...Jacomo Ungaro, cutter of letters and inhabitant of this most excellent city for forty years, having discovered the way to print measured music, and fearing that others, as happens, may reap the fruit of his labors, begs your Excellency that you be pleased to grant him the favor that no one else may print or have printed the said measured music either in this city or in its provinces for the next fifteen years, nor bring books printed elsewhere to sell in this city or subordinate lands, under penalty of losing all the books and 100 ducats for every time that it occurs.[25]

The presence of a professional music typecutter in Venice for forty years encourages a hypothesis that places the process of type design in the hands of such an individual rather than with individual printers. Such an explanation is supported by the appearance in Petrucci's type of a flat sign that had been used by Hamman in 1498 (type G1, *Agenda pataviensis*) and a pausa remarkably like Petrucci's in the 1480 type of Theodor of Würzburg

(M1, Niger's *Grammatica*). It also supplies an explanation for the claim in Petrucci's original privilege of 1498 that, in addition to protection of a new way to print mensural music, it would provide protection of a way to make the printing of chant much easier. Petrucci did not print chant, but Ungaro was likely the creator of chant types as well as mensural types. A monopoly system to protect types as well as titles contributes to centralized control of music publication and distribution, and it was already in place in the fifteenth century.

The desire to reduce the number of designs of manuscript music cast into metal type had a serious impact on the appearance of printed complex neumes necessary for melismatic passages over one syllable of text. Such neumes, which are made up of ascending and descending parts, were often broken into parts to be cast in metal. The greatest skill on the part of the typecutter, typecaster and music compositor was required to create and set types in snugly abutting fashion to conceal breaks from the reader. A comparison of four settings of the melismatic "Ecce lignum" of Good Friday illustrates several treatments of complex neumes over single syllables, although the passages do not quite agree on the melody and text underlay. The first printed missal of ca. 1472 with printed text underlay and manuscript music contains neumes of two to five notes clearly laid out over a text carefully broken into syllables with the assistance of single, double, and half bar lines (see Fig. 3a). In the first printed version of the chant in the 1476 missal of Ulrich Han (Fig. 3b) neumes have been broken up and notes are too widely spaced since with the exception of the lozenge music types do not abut each other. There are not enough designs to represent the notation (diagonal, torculus). Despite the compositor's clear effort to tie the text to particular neumes, the melody is not tightly linked to the text. Emerich (Fig. 3d) supplies diagonals of varying stem lengths, a torculus for "mundi" and abutting sorts to link notes over one syllable (cru-cis). An awareness of the inadequacy of his quarto type of 1494 is apparent in the addition in the octavo type of 1498 of new designs for a clivis of a descending third preceding the last note and a three-note scandicus (Ve-ni-te). A final example by Pachel (Fig. 3c) illustrates a problematic reading produced by types for complex neumes that do not abut each other; text underlay is unclear.

A broader spectrum of music printing is presented in Fig. 4 which includes printing from woodcuts and gothic notation. Johann Emerich of Speier's first music (Fig. 4a) was cut in wood, a tour de force for a woodcut artist but not easily legible to the reader, especially since note stems are on the left instead of the right. Stephan Planck used Han's music type for a folio missal in 1482 and a quarto missal in 1488 (Fig. 4b); the wrong clef, poor underlay, and broken neumes leave much to be desired. Bevilaqua's longstemmed type (Fig. 4d) looks lost with the text underlay below the rubrics. Pinzi's text underlay in 1494 (Fig. 4e) is also unsatisfactory: it is unclear on which side of the virga the stem belongs. The example by Arrivabene (Fig. 4c) is a pleasure to read for the careful composition of neumes and text underlay as well as for the well cut types with variable stem length, though the nested staves do not tightly abut. The three examples of the same melody for the Kyrie in gothic plainchant notation illustrate an assortment of clearly defined neumes of quite different design that match the gothic textura text types with which they are set.

The earliest staves to be printed in a first impression beneath music type were cast as entire lines (1473 *Graduale*, 1476 *Missale romanum*), but as they too were later cast in large equal segments or small nested segments set by a proliferation of compositors of uneven ability, gaps between segments became common. Of course, the printers who inserted staves into cheaper publications never meant for printed type had little concern for exactness and often used wavy metal rules or woodcuts that were a distinct challenge to the music scribe. Such shortcuts were probably a shrewd evaluation of the market since no music was ever written in many of the extant copies despite the fact that only the most attractive copies survive today, often because owners were able to afford painted initials and handsome bindings. The buyer of an inexpensive Venetian octavo missal may have been a priest unable to write plainchant or even to read it. There were no seminaries in the fifteenth century to train the secular clergy whose names are inscribed in some copies and the state of Latin literacy itself was so low that concerned church leaders complained that "scarcely two in a hundred or perhaps ten in a thousand can be found who can read the daily services".[26]

Only one of the illustrations of "Ecce lignum" included a flat where necessary above "salus" (Fig. 3a), the rest relying on the rules of musica ficta by which trained singers knew where accidentals belonged. In Emerich's gradual (1499/1500) the editor Franciscus de Brugis remarked in the preface that "we French, the Germans, and those who live in the neighboring regions delight in B natural. The Italians and other nations on this side of the mountains prefer B flat."[27] Nearly every copy of that gradual has accidentals added in manuscript, stamped, printed, covered by white ink, or scraped off the vellum, evidence of the controversial decisions made by the international committee attempting reform of the chant. Emerich cast a B flat for R18 (1494) and R19 (1496), no accidentals for the octavo format R20 (1498), and forms of the B flat and B natural for the choir-book format R21(M). No other Italian missal types include accidentals

a.

b.

c.

d.

Figure 3 "Ecce lignum," Good Friday.

(a) *Missale romanum*. [Central Italy, ca. 1472].

(b) *Missale romanum*. Rome: Ulrich Han, 12 X 1476.

(c) *Missale romanum*. Milan: Leonard Pachel, 16 IV 1499.

(d) *Missale romanum*. Venice: Johann Emerich of Speier, 10 X 1497.

Figure 4 "Ite missa est" and "Kyrie eleyson."

(a) *Missale romanum*. Venice: Johann Emerich of Speier, 28 IV 1493.

(b) *Missale romanum*. Rome: Stephan Planck, 22 XII 1488.

(c) *Missale romanum*. Venice: Giorgio Arrivabene, 29 V 1499.

(d) *Missale romanum*. Venice: Simone Gabi, called Bevilaqua 10 III 1499.

(e) *Missale romanum*. Venice: Filippo Pinzi, 29 III 1494.

(f) *Missale misnense*. [Speier: Peter Drach, ca. 1498].

(g) *Missale argentinense*. [Strasbourg: Johann Prüss, 1490].

(h) *Missale augustanum*. [Bamberg]: Johann Sensenschmidt and Johann Beckenhub, 10 I 1489.

though most German missal types have a B flat (folio types of Michael Wenssler, Johann Pfeyll, Peter Schoeffer, Erhard Ratdolt, Johann Petri, Johann Sensenschmidt, Georg Reyser). The tendencies toward centralization and standardization associated with printing and international distribution would assist in a transition toward written accidentals in the same way they encouraged written-out textual abbreviations in printed books.

The opposite trend occurred with liquescent or ornamental neumes. True, such neumes were cut into type in the fifteenth century for use by many printers, but they have disappeared from chant books today. Certainly traditions of notating liquescence varied enormously from region to region. A decorated longa here called a virga cum orisco was common in Italy and was included in more than half of the Roman and Ambrosian types used there in the fifteenth century (see Fig. 5). Each type had only one design for the note although manuscript notation had varied the shape according to the melodic ornamentation required.[28] The virga cum orisco appears at the beginning or end of the chant and may have been associated with the practice of intonation as the singer sought a higher or lower pitch, lengthening and decorating the note accordingly.

Other liquescent notes in fifteenth-century types (see Fig. 6) suggest descending or ascending ornamentation of internal neumes. The localized performance traditions associated with such signs have gradually disappeared, but the fact that they were cut into metal is evidence that they

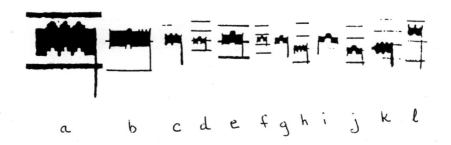

Figure 5 Virga cum orisco

(a) Moilli, R2; (b) Emerich of Speier, R21, (c) Scoto, R3; (d) Gabi, called Bevilaqua, R8; (e) Hamman, R9; (f) Hamman, R10; (g) Pinzi, R17; (h) Emerich of Speier, R18; (i) Torresani, R3; (j) Arrivabene, R25; (k) Bonini, R31; (l) Valdarfer, A1.

were important at the time. Since such designs indicated ornamentation of another note, they had to be printed in close association with that note. Emerich was skilled in kerned types whose faces could overlap adjacent types, and his small liquescent notes are a superb example of the technique (see Fig. 6f).

The mensural Credo was important enough in the plainchant tradition of the fifteenth century that two fonts were modified to allow publication of black mensural notation. Both the 1477 and 1499/1500 Italian graduals included the mensural Credo, and Emerich's type had designs cast specifically for the time signature, semibreve, minim, and semiminim.

The techniques of designing music types and composing them in formes that were developed for printing the hundreds of editions of missals that were published in the fifteenth century prepared the way for the modest appearance of a few dozen editions of secular music in the next decades of the sixteenth century. As manuscript music was transformed into type in liturgical books, type designers confronted the relationship of letters and note heads, lines of alphabetic characters and music staves, a first impression of a regular set of staff lines, and finally the formidable challenge of printing designs on any line or space of that staff in a second impression. Editorial control by scholar or committee, systems of privileges to protect titles, types, or genres, international standardization of notational practice, and increasing attention to a single correct text are practices that, once introduced, became taken for granted in the publishing world; and

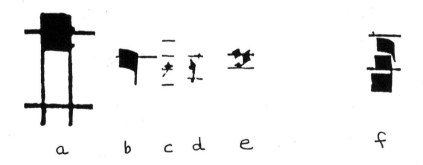

Figure 6 Liquescent neumes in fifteenth-century plainchant type.

(a) Moilli R2, (b) Emerich of Speier, R21; (c) [Prüss]; (d) Valdarfer, A1; (e) Reyser; (f) a kerned liquescent note, Emerich of Speier, R21.

music became a truly international language. As the tyranny of the locked rectangular forme, and metal type are replaced by other forms of music printing in the twentieth century, it may be useful to reconsider the musical practices that were lost and gained in the shift in printing technology of the fifteenth century.

ABBREVIATIONS

GW   *Gesamtkatalog der Wiegendrucke*. Vols. 1–8:1. Leipzig: K. W. Hiersemann, 1925–1940. Vols. 8:1–9:2. Stuttgart: A. Hiersemann, 1968–1985.

H   Ludwig Hain. *Repertorium bibliographicum, In quo libri omnes ab arte typographica inventa usque ad annum MD*. 2 vols. Stuttgart: J. G. Cotta, 1826–1838.

C   Walter Arthur Copinger. *Supplement to Hain's Repertorium bibliographicum*. Parts 1–2:1–2 London: H. Sotheran & Co., 1895–1902.

Goff   Frederick R. Goff. *Incunabula in American Libraries: A Third Census of Fifteenth-Century Books Recorded in North American Collections*. Millwood, N.Y.: Kraus Reprint, 1973.

Proctor   Robert Proctor. *An Index to the Early Printed Books in the British Museum: from the Invention of Printing of the Year 1500. With notes of those in the Bodleian Library*. 2 vols. and supplements. Registers by Konrad Burger. London: Kegan Paul; Trench; Trübner & Co., 1898–1906.

Endnotes

1   The definition used by Kathi Meyer-Baer for her *Liturgical Music Incunabula: A Descriptive Catalogue* (London: The Bibliographical Society, 1962). Despite her statement that her 257 numbered items involve the printing of music (p. xxxviii), some numbered items (for example, number 34) contain space for manuscript music. The more recent study of fifteenth-century printed music by Maria Przywecka-Samecka (*Początki Drukarstwa Muzycznego w Europie Wiek XV*, Prace Wrocławskiego Towarzystwa Naukowego, Sera A. Nr. 221 [Wrocław; Wydawnictwo Polskiej Akademii Nauk, 1981]) lists only those incunabula with printed music. See also discussion in Mary Kay Duggan, *Italian Music Incunabula: Printers and Types* (Berkeley, CA: University of California Press, 1992), 14–15.

2 Duggan, *Italian Music Incunabula*, Table 3. Helmut Rosing's estimate of 1,500 incunabula with printed music seems unlikely. Helmut Rosing and Joachim Schlichte, "Die Serie A/I des RISM: Eine Dokumentation der Musikdrucke von den Anfängen bis 1800," *Gutenberg-Jahrbuch* (1983): 132.

3 For a bibliographical description of each and information on copies, see numbers 23 to 141* of Duggan, *Italian Music Incunabula*, part III.

4 Three small octavo editions of the *Missale romanum*: Venice: Franz Renner, 1481 H 11366, Goff M-6589), and Milan: Leonard Pachel and Ulrich Scinzenzeller, 1483 (C 4196); Venice: Giovanni de' Gregori, Gregorio de' Gregori, Giacomo Britannico, and Antonio Stanchi 1483 (C 4192). The lack of music in the *Missale romanum* printed in Glagolitic ([Kosinj? Venice?], 1483; Goff M–695) probably reflects the state of the copytext, since liturgical music for the Slavonic service has a performance tradition that is still transmitted orally today (see Josip Andreis, *Music in Croatia*, trans. Vladimir Ivir [Zagreb: Institute of Musicology, 1974], 19). Music also would not be expected in the abbreviated missal called a *Missale speciale* (Venice: [Johann Emerich of Speier for] Luca Antonio Giunta for Christopher Thum, 1500 or 1504; Proctor 13104).

5 The best list of editions of the missal printed in the fifteenth century remains Hanns Bohatta's revision of William Henry James Weale's *Bibliographia liturgica. Catalogus missalium ritus latini ab anno M. CCCC. LXXV. Impressorum* (London: B. Quaritch, 1928).

6 J. Linneborn, *Die Reformation der westfälischer Benedictiner-Klöster im 15. Jahrhundert durch die Bursfelder Congregation* (Brünn: Raigerner Benedictiner-Buchdruckerei, 1899); Barbara Franks, "Subiaco, ein Reformkonvent des späten Mittelalters," *Quellen und Forschungen aus italienischen Archiven und Bibliotheken* 52 (1972): 619–55; Virgil Redlich, *Tegernsee und die deutsche Geistesgeschichte im 15. Jahrhundert*, 1931, reprint by Scientia Verlag Aalen, 1974 (Schriftenreihe zur Bayerischen Landesgeschichte. Herausgegeben von der Kom. für bayerische Landesgeschichte bei der Bayerischen Akademie der Wissenschaften, 9); Luigi Pesce, *Ludovico Barbo, vescovo di Treviso, 1437–1443. Cura pastorale, riforma della chiesa, spiritualità* (Italia sacra, 9–10) (1969); Tommaso Leccisotti, "Il 'Missale monasticum secundum morem et ritum casinensis congregationis alias Sancte Iustine'", in *Miscellanea Giovanni Mercati* (Vatican City: Biblioteca Apostolica Vaticana, 1946) (Studi e Testi, 125), 5:363–75; K. Holter, "Der Einfluss der Melker Reform auf das klösterliche Buchwesen in Osterreich," in *Klösterliche Sachkultur des Spätmittelalters, Internationaler Kongress Krems an der Donau 18. bis 21. September 1978* (Oesterreichische Akademie der Wissenschaften. Philosophisch-historische Klasse, Sitzungsberichte Bd. 367) (Vienna: Oesterreichische Akademie der Wissenschaften, 1980), 305–20.

7 Paulus Volk, *Urkunden zur Geschichte der Bursfelder Kongregation* (Bonn: Ludwig Röhrscheid Verlag, 1951) (Kanonistische Studien und Texte, Band 20), document 10, 70–71.

8 Volk, *Urkunden*, document 17, 82–84.

9 Suitbert Bäumer, *Geschichte des Breviers: Versuch einer quellenmässigen Darstellung der Entwicklung des altkirchlichen und des römischen Officiums bis auf unsere Tage* (Freiburg im Breisgau Herder 1895), 379.

10 Gabriele Paolo Carosi, *Da Magonza a Subiaco: l'introduzione della stampa in Italia* (Busta Arsizio: Bramante, 1982), 69.

11 Despite the reform of the liturgy in printed Roman missals, owners of individual copies

could insert manuscript additions as desired, as in the fifty-three leaves of sequences for the liturgical year added to the octavo *Missale romanum* printed in Venice; by Nikolaus von Frankfurt in 1485 (Library of Congress, Washington, D.C., Batchelder Collection).

12   Vatican City, Biblioteca Vaticana, Inc. IV. 29, provenance, S. Silvestro al Quirinale, Rome. For details, see Duggan, *Italian Music Incunabula*, part III, Descriptive Bibliography, no. 105.

13   Such a committee from both sides of the Alps that resorted to singing passages under dispute is mentioned in the preface to the *Graduale Romanum* printed by Johann Emerich of Speier for Luca Antonio Giunta in Venice in 1499 (H 7844, Goff G-332); reprinted in Giuseppe Massera, *La "Mano musicale perfetta" de Francesco de Brugis dalle prefazioni ai corali di L. A. Giunta (Venezia: 1499–1504)* (Florence: Leo S. Olschki, 1963) (Historiae Musicae Cultores Biblioteca 18), 71–73.

14   Aimé-Georges Martimort, "Missels incunables d'origine franciscaine," in *Mélanges liturgiques offert au R. P. Dom Bernard Botte, O.S.B., de l'Abbaye du Mont César* (Louvain: Abbaye du Mont César, 1972), no. 1; Duggan, *Italian Music Incunabula*, no. 38.

15   Luigi Michelini Tocci, "Incunaboli sconosciuti e incunaboli mal conosciuti della Biblioteca Vaticana," in *Studi di biliografia e di storia in onore di Tammaro de Marinis*, 3 vols. (Verona: Stampa Valdonega, 1964), 3:189–99, 214–15, plates XIX, XXI–XXII.

16   Mary Kay Duggan, "The Design of the Early Printed Missal," *Journal of the Printing Historical Society* no. 22 (1993), 72-75.

17   Duggan, *Italian Music Incunabula*, Table 1 and Map 1. Michel Huglo, *Fonti e paleografia del canto ambrosiano* (Milan: Scuola Tipografica di San Benedetto, 1956) (Archivio Ambrosiano 7), map on 111. For Messine-German, see the introduction to *Missale notatum strigoniense ante 1431 in Posonio*, ed. Janka Szendrei and Richard Rybaric (Budapest, 1982), 46–67.

18   Redlich, *Tegernsee und die deutsche Geistesgeschichte*, 151 and document 15.

19   Daniel Heartz, *Pierre Attaingnant, Royal Printer of Music* (Berkeley: University of California Press, 1969), 57–58.

20   Duggan, *Italian Music Incunabula*, figs. 14–15.

21   Ibid., 26–33, figs. 6–12. For an illustration of single and double impression punches, matrices, and type for music, see H. Edmund Poole, "Printing Music from Type," in *Music Printing and Publishing*, ed. D. W. Krummel and Stanley Sadie (New York: W. W. Norton, 1990) (The Norton/Grove Handbooks in Music), plate 2, 19.

22   For a directory of types, see, ibid., 182–84, and individual type specimens, part 2.

23   Mary Kay Duggan, "A System for Describing Fifteenth-Century Music Type," *Gutenberg-Jahrbuch* (1984): table 2.

24   Duggan, *Italian Music Incunabula*, fig. 56.

25   Ibid., 38–41; for original Italian, see app. 1, 301.

26   Rev. Giustiniani and Querini, *Libellus ad Leonem Decem* (Venice, 1513), as quoted in Denis Hay, *The Church in Italy in the Fifteenth Century* (London: Cambridge University Press, 1977), 62.

27   "Gallici enim nostri: et qui Germanias incolunt omnesque alii eas circa regiones duro maxime delectantur. Italici vero et cetere nationes citra illos montes molli magis alliciuntur." Reprinted in Massera, *La "Mano musicale"*, 71.

28   Duggan, *Italian Music Incunabula*, fig. 2a–b: Antiphonal, Archivio di San Pietro, Perugia, Ms. L, examples of liquescent neumes.

International Dissemination of Printed Music During the Second Half of the Eighteenth Century

SARAH ADAMS

Cornell University

The traditional view of the music publishing scene during the second half of the eighteenth century seriously underestimates the international character of this commerce and the extent of business transactions between publishers. My research, which involves tracing a specific repertory across Europe, has led to new comprehension of the music publishing trade, especially with respect to the dissemination of music. Evidence in publishers' catalogues, advertisements in contemporary periodicals, correspondence, and research into publishing houses makes it clear that, to a greater extent than has been realized, the market for printed music was international.[1] The music trade of the second half of the eighteenth century encompassed wide dissemination of music that was not limited to the most famous composers, nor random or haphazard, and depended on well-established distribution networks and business arrangements between publishers. This article will survey this evidence, describe some of the routes a composition took on its way to being published, and, by way of conclusion, touch on some of the larger issues raised by a more complete knowledge of musical dissemination.

****

International distribution of printed music has traditionally been associated more closely with the nineteenth than the eighteenth century and is generally connected with composers' control over the publication of their music. During the nineteenth century it became common for composers to arrange simultaneous publication of a work in different countries. For example, in connection with J. N. Hummel's multiple publication of his music in London, Paris, and somewhere in Germany or Austria, Joel Sachs notes "the highly developed state of the publishing industry" and hypothesizes "the web of international publishing was, by the 1820s, already well-spun."[2] Modern descriptions of the music trade during the early decades of the nineteenth century describe its hitherto unequalled growth and expansion, due both to technological advances and to increased public demand, which facilitated importation between countries.[3] This new public demand led to the appearance of famous composers' works in numerous cities in close succession, as mentioned above. In fact, however, aspects of such descriptions also apply to music publishing of the late eighteenth century. This period can also be regarded as a turning point in the history of music publishing, a time during which music printing techniques improved due to the extensive use of engraving, music began to be circulated more frequently in printed rather than manuscript form, a large number of publishers went into business, and the public indicated increasing interest and demand.

The influence of the business world on the creation and dissemination of music cannot be ignored. Book historians have already recognized the importance of publishing and have begun to document the extent of the international book trade during the eighteenth century. According to John Feather, eighteenth-century

> "publishers did not merely organize the production of books, but also, crucially, their distribution. . . . Complex patterns of book distribution were developed; and the international book trade, which had existed since the fifteenth century, grew rapidly as books moved between countries, despite the impediments imposed by customs officers and censors."[4]

Similar conditions may well have applied to music distribution; there was considerable overlap between the book and music industries both in methods of dissemination and, more obviously, by the fact that some firms published both books and music.

Although many musicologists have described connections between a given publisher and others, a comprehensive account of eighteenth-century European music publishing has yet to be written. Traditional accounts emphasize "piracy" (or unauthorized reprinting), and the travels of individual composers as the primary means of dissemination. These accounts also stress the isolation of certain areas from active trade which discouraged music dissemination by "legal" means, with the exception of certain known connections like that between Mannheim and Paris. Because of the multitude of eighteenth-century editions, establishing the authenticity of sources has always been an important issue. Therefore, "inauthentic" prints and reprints have not received a great deal of attention; their value for understanding dissemination and publishing practices has not been recognized.

Because existing research on distribution of music usually concentrates on works of a single composer, the output of a single publisher, or practices within a single country, no overall view has emerged. To my knowledge no one has studied the transmission of an entire repertory across composers throughout Europe.[5] I have traced the works of an entire repertory, quartets and quintets for mixed groups of wind and string instruments, through publishers' catalogues of approximately the last third of the eighteenth century, from England, France, Germany, Austria, and Holland.[6] Evidence of dissemination of this repertory between cities and countries, as well as evidence in catalogues, correspondence and other sources, supports the hypothesis that many of the major publishing houses not only had connections and publishing agreements with each other, but also networks of agents in other mayor cities selling music on commission. There is overlap in all domains: from publisher to publisher within the same city, from city to city within a country, and between countries. Though a small proportion of the works were published once by a single publisher, most of them, and not only those by the most famous composers, were offered for sale by more than one publisher or music dealer and sometimes were printed by several publishers. The wide dissemination is exemplified by a composer such as Pleyel. André published his first three flute quartets (B. 381–383) in 1789; within the next twenty or more years they were published by one other German publisher, and two from Vienna, four from Paris, four from London, one from Amsterdam, all in addition to wide dissemination in manuscript copies.[7] Such examples are common in the mixed quartet and quintet repertory, and most likely in numerous other repertories as well. Evidence of such widespread dissemination, especially between publishers in different countries, warrants further examination of the international trade.

****

Antoine Perrin's 1781 *Almanach de la librairie* (first published in 1777 as the *Manuel de l'auteur et du librairie*) proves to be a rich source for musicology.[8] It appears to have been a combination business manual and address book, containing detailed information on rules and regulations of the trade, and lists of Parisian and provincial publishers, as well as those from the principal cities in Europe. It includes close to 1100 names for Paris and the French provinces, and well over 800 names in 231 locations from elsewhere in Europe. The locations in the non-French list range as widely as Moscow, St. Petersburg, Prague, Warsaw, Stockholm, and Lisbon, in addition to all of the expected cities in England and Germany. Some of the names are immediately recognizable to scholars of eighteenth-century music: Breitkopf in Leipzig, Lotter in Augsburg, Castaud in Lyon, Westphal in Hamburg. Others are less well-known today but also had connections with the music world: for example, Gerle in Prague and Hartknoch in Riga. Owners of this book could have used it as a means of establishing foreign contacts, both for exporting their own stock and importing that of the foreign dealers; the foreign listings and those in the provinces) even indicate departure times of the stagecoach from Paris.

A 1785 advertisement published in the *Staats- und gelehrte Zeitung des hamburgischen unpartheyischen Correspondenten* for the subscription series of the Viennese music publisher Franz Anton Hoffmeister includes a long list of his agents from sixty-six cities in Europe (mostly from Germany, northern, and eastern Europe–it excludes France and England).[9] More than half of the sixty-six names (or businesses) from Hoffmeister's list are included in the 1777 or the 1781 *Almanach*. A later section of the 1781 *Almanach* lists the names and addresses of the *Marchands de musique* and music engravers in Paris and the provinces, as well as in foreign countries (Castaud of Lyons is listed both here and in the book dealer list). It also nearly duplicates a list of foreign merchants that had appeared during the 1770's in the Parisian music periodical *Almanach musical*.

It is no accident that an international trade directory of such magnitude was published in France; Paris was the leading center of music publication for much of the eighteenth century. During the 1760s and 1770s more music seems to have been published in Paris than in all other European cities taken together.[10] The Breitkopf thematic catalogues for this time listed Parisian prints more often than those from any other city but, especially towards the later part of the century, many of the composers represented by the Parisian prints were not French. Mozart and Haydn both were first printed in Paris, Haydn's Op. 1 Quartets in 1764 by La Chevardière and Mozart's early violin and keyboard sonatas also in 1764. Music from German composers was in demand not only in France but also in England. Indeed, one of the most striking aspects of the French and English publishers' catalogues is the abundance of foreign composers in comparison with native ones. Anik Devriès concurs with this observation and identifies a turning point for this trend in Paris: the majority of the composers represented before 1740 were French; after that date, the majority were Italian and German.[11] The publisher Le Clerc, for example, reversed the proportions of French composers to foreigners: in his later catalogues only about one dozen French composers remain, compared to many more Italian, German, Flemish and English composers. Devriès observes the same phenomenon with La Chevardière, Venier, Le Menu, Huberty, Sieber, Le Duc, Imbault and Pleyel. Similarly, in England native composers were represented in vocal music (songs, catches, glees, though not opera), but Germans and Austrians ruled the instrumental categories.

The industry in Paris was better developed and supported more composers than in other cities (later, London was an exception). It was common for composers to go to Paris to enhance their reputations; often they preferred to have their music printed there as well, for reasons of economics and convenience. This letter from Mozart to his father in 1777 about a projected trip to Paris doubtless reflects the attitude of many composers at the time: "Wendling assures that I shall never regret it. He has been twice to Paris.... He maintains that it is still the only place where one can make money and a great reputation."[12] Wendling told Mozart that "you can get sonatas, trios and quartets engraved *Par souscription*. [Christian] Cannabich and [Joseph Toeschi] send a great deal of their music to Paris." In a later letter Mozart complained that Mannheim is "a miserly spot, and the engraver will not do them [6 clavier sonatas] at his own expense, but wants to go halves with me in the sale. So I prefer to have them engraved in Paris, where the engravers are delighted to get something new and pay handsomely and where it is easier to get a thing done by subscription."[14] Similarly, Dittersdorf indicated in his autobiography the ease with which a foreign composer could remain at home and send his works on to Paris to have them printed: "Orders were sent directly to me from Paris concerning the majority of my compositions."[15]

Contemporary French journals are rich sources for descriptions of European musical life and the interest in Paris for music from foreign countries. The *Journal de musique* claimed, in its first issue in 1770, that one of its five sections would be devoted to announcements of new works, both from France and foreign countries. The editors hoped for international distribution of their journal and stated in the introduction that "in order to fully attain this objective we are open to communications with Italy, Spain, Germany, and England. We dare to hope that this journal will be well received every country."[16] The *Calendrier musical universel* from 1788–89 includes "notice of musical works performed in Paris, at Versailles, at Saint-Cloud, in various European theaters such as those of

London, Vienna, Saint Petersburg, and of the principal Italian cities."[17] The 1780 catalogue of the Mannheim publisher Götz proves that these publications attained international readership: he advertised the 1775, 1776, 1777 and 1778 issues of the *Almanach musical* and the 1777 *Journal de musique* for sale.

A notice in a 1777 issue of the *Journal de musique* acknowledges the difficulty "amateurs of good music" have in obtaining Italian music since it is not printed and must be copied by hand, which takes a long time and therefore "harms the progress of art." They announce a service which will supply the best Italian music:

> We believe, therefore, that we do music-lovers a service and give them interesting news by announcing that a valuable collection of Italian scores and over 400 new arias of the best masters, such as Anfossi, Piccini, Maïo, Sacchini, Paisiello, etc., has been established at the Bureau of the *Journal de musique,* rue Montmartre, next to that of the Vieux Augustins. Copies can be procured at the usual price, and, in order for the outcome of this announcement to be a success, we will continue to send for the new works which are the most applauded in the various Italian theaters, therefore forming a unique kind of library, comprised of all that there is of the best of foreign music, which will be communicated with haste to all who wish it. The price of these copies is set at 4 francs per page.[18]

Of particular interest in this announcement is the description of a library containing the best foreign works. Those in charge of this collection most likely had arrangements with foreign composers, publishers, and distributors .

A list in the *Almanach musical* entitled "Marchands de musique" divides music sellers into two classes:

> Publishers are those who print works of music and who only carry the music of their stock. Merchants are those who do not limit themselves to music from their own stock and keep a selection of works of assorted composers, publishers, and of other merchants.[19]

The list of publishers in the 1779 issue includes 31 in Paris. There are 8 Paris merchants listed, 52 merchants "En Province" and 14 from foreign countries. These are:

Augsbourg	M.M. Lotter
	Rieger, Libraire
Bruxelles	Godefroy
	Pris & Van-Ypen. rue de la Madeleine
Francfort	Otto, Organiste
Hambourg	Huer
	J.C. Westphal & Compagnie
Londres	Bremmer vis-à-vis Somersethouse dans le Strand
	Longman & Luckey, Cheapside
	Napier
	Veuve Welcher, rue Ste Anne
	Welcher le fils, rue Catherine dans le Strand
Mannheim	Goëtz & Compagnie
Vienne	Artaria & Compagnie

The implications are that the new music announced in the journal would be available from these businesses and that the journal strove for and most likely had international readership. Furthermore, the efficiency of the communications network is impressive: several of these businesses appear on the list within a few years of establishing business. Artaria is listed during the second year of their existence as a music publisher (although they had imported foreign prints since 1776) and Napier, who began business in 1772, by 1775 was included in the *Almanach*. Westphal's first (extant) catalogue appeared in 1770 and in 1773 his business was included in the *Journal de musique* as an establishment where one could find the new items announced in the journal.

The international flavor of such announcements is not limited to the later eighteenth century, however. As early as 1728 Francois Bouvin, a Paris merchant, advertised in the *Mercure de France* that one could find in his shop "every kind of beautiful composition, both French [and] Latin prints and engravings, as well as Italian and others of the best authors, also Dutch engravings; and that he will offer them as cheaply as he can, almost at cost."[20] In 1734, the prominent music publisher Le Clerc announced his "general catalogue of music printed or engraved in France. Included with this is music printed in foreign countries which is available now. 1734. It is for sale in Paris at le Sieur Leclerc."[21]

Imports like these were not limited to France. Estienne Roger of Amsterdam announced in 1703 that his publications could be had in

London at the shop of Francois and Paul Vaillant. In 1712 he advertised that one could purchase his prints

> à Londres chez Henry Ribotteau, à Berlin chez A. Dussarat, à Hall chez A. Selluis, à Liège chez Herman Delmeer, à Cologne chez P. Poner, à Bruxelles chez Joseph Serstevens, marchands librairies, et à Hambourg chez Jean Chrestian Schickhardt, fameux componiste.[22]

Advertisements in London also reflected business transactions with foreign publishers. For example, a Robert Bremner advertisement in the *Public Advertiser* during the 1760s for music from La Chevardière announces:

> In 2 vol. for the year 1764, 1765. Price of each stitched 12s. Le Journal Hebdomadaire: Being a collection of the most favorite French songs, from the French Comic Operas, for the Voice and Harpsichord, with an Accompaniment for the Violin. Printed at Paris: and sold by R. Bremner. Where may be had, just imported, Above two hundred different works.[23]

Another advertisement, from 1769, describes a list of works "just imported from Holland and France" that includes works by Boccherini, Kloffers, Graff, Reinard, Nardini, Toeschi, Cannabich, Stamitz, Gossec, Holzbauer, Beck, Wagenseil and Schwindel and concludes, exhaustively, "with many other works too tedious to mention."[24] Bremner's source in Amsterdam was most likely Hummel, from whom he acquired Haydn's Op. 1 quartets in 1765 and other Haydn works.[25]

Even though none of the German or Austrian cities constituted major music publishing centers at this time, they participated in the widespread international trade. The 1778 *Almanach de la librairie* lists German shops from 82 cities. The book fairs held annually in Leipzig and Frankfurt were attended not only by representatives from all over Germany but from foreign countries as well; those who dealt in music also attended. Breitkopf established contacts with both composers and publishers; he offered not only a wide selection of manuscript copies but foreign prints from London, Paris, Amsterdam and other cities. What is not yet fully appreciated, however, is that his example was not an exception in Germany–there were other publishers (or sellers) who contracted widely. In addition, we do not yet know enough about the dealers who sold works mainly of other publishers and ran musical warehouses. Some of the figures who deserve more attention with this in mind include Johann Michael Götz, Johann

Christoph Westphal, and Johann David Otto. Copy houses like that of Johann Traeg in Vienna often dealt in foreign prints; Traeg also ran a music lending library.[26]

Johann Michael Götz, who eventually engraved his own prints, published a 106-page catalogue in 1780 consisting mainly of foreign prints, though there is a section of manuscript music near the end. Most of the prints originate from Paris, but there are others from Amsterdam, Brussels, London, Offenbach, Bonn, Wolfenbüttel, Magdebourg, Vienna, Nürnberg, Braunschweig, Lyon, Frankfurt, Mannheim, Augsburg, Berlin, Riga, Geneva, Le Hague, etc. Equally diverse geographically is the selection found in the catalogues of Johann Christoph Westphal from Hamburg. His 1782 catalogue is 287 pages long. (He was included both in the *Almanach de la librairie* book dealer index and the *Almanach musical* foreign music seller list.) In addition to the cities mentioned in connection with Götz he advertised prints from St. Petersburg, Venice, and Prague, among others. He must have had an arrangement with Breitkopf, since several of his catalogues include a section entitled "Manuscript Articles from Breitkopf's Publishing House." He also offered for sale Breitkopf's thematic catalogues and those from the Hummel firm in Amsterdam. Johann David Otto, who was one of the Frankfurt agents for Hummel, was another music dealer clearly well-established in international trading; he announced his connection with Hummel in 1758.[27] In 1760 he announced that his stock contained works of publishers from Nürnberg, Amsterdam, Berlin, Braunschweig, and Augsburg, and he soon added works from abroad: Paris in 1764 and London in 1768. These tantalizing details alone hint at the need for further examination.

* * * * * * * * * * *

Having established the widespread nature of the international music trade in a general sense, let us now consider three of the various means by which a piece of music might come to be published. The first and the simplest was the direct route from composer to publisher, which is familiar to us from Haydn's career after 1780. The chance for a composer to have a greater say in how and where a work was published must have been an attractive option. Other composers of the day engaged in this practice: Paul Wranitzky in Vienna wrote to the London publisher Bland in 1790 (Haydn carried the letter to London), asking if Bland would publish his work:

> I asked you in my first letter about three completely new quintets or 6 quatuors concertants–if you wished to publish one or the other–because I would like to be known in London. Mr. Hayden knows the quintets. Tomorrow morning Mr. Salomon will do me the honor of coming here in order to hear the quartets, and he will speak to you.[28]

Dittersdorf wrote to Artaria in 1788 offering the string quartets he had just composed:

> Now–I offer you the original manuscript or, more accurately, my own score of them for the same price you paid for Mozart's and in addition for the first ten prints or copies, and I am certain that you will do better with mine than you did with Mozart's (which, indeed, I and still greater theorists consider to deserve the highest praise, but which because of their overwhelming and unrelenting artfulness are not to everyone's taste).[29]

A different method of establishing direct contact was suggested by C. P. E Bach, who wrote to the Hamburg organist J. J. H. Westphal asking him to come to him directly to purchase his works instead of obtaining them from dealers.[30]

A second route for a musical work to take to a publisher was via an agent. Many of the larger publishing houses had agents in other cities, both to sell music and to facilitate acquisition of new music to send back for publication. Some agents were employed by only one publisher under contract to obtain music for them; an example is Griesinger's arrangement with Breitkopf & Härtel. Others had looser arrangements with one or several publishers, either selling their music on commission or providing them with music from their own stock. For example, Traeg was an agent for Breitkopf & Hartel in Vienna, J. Otto was the Frankfurt agent for Hummel, as well as for André, Pichl was the Viennese correspondent to Pleyel, Paul Wranitzky was the Viennese agent for André; there are many more. Various English publishers issued statements like the following: "Instrumental music printed and sold by J. Bland at his Music Warehouse...may be had at all Music and Booksellers in Great Britain and by the Principal Music Dealers on the Continent."[31] J.J. Hummel both imported music and had agents abroad for the sale of his own publications; shops in Stockholm advertised Hummel works as early as 1769–70.[32] Similar announcements appear on his catalogues from Amsterdam. From 1762: "One finds (here) free catalogs of a great deal of foreign music, printed in Paris, London, and in Germany"; and from 1771: "This catalogue is distributed (for) free by the above- mentioned and by the correspondents."[33] In the 7 October 1789 issue of *Musikalische Realzeitung*, Hr. Cantor Bißmann of Frankfurt am Main advertised that he had new music from André, and on 24 February 1790 that new music from Hummel's firm could be had from him. On 2 June 1790 he ran the following advertisement: "Herr Cantor Bißmann and company in Frankfurt am Main sell, in addition to music on commission of publishers from Berlin, Mannheim, Speyr, Offenbach, and elsewhere, also genuine Romansch violin strings . . ."[34] Until 1800 André had agents (in addition to Vienna, and probably also London and Paris) in Amsterdam, Augsburg, Basel, Frankfurt, Gotha, Hamburg, Köln, Kopenhagen, Munich, Rotterdam, St. Gallen & Straßburg (he increased the number after 1800).[35] Hoffmeister's 1785 list of agents included those from

> Augsburg, Anspach, Amsterdam, Bern, Braunschweig, Breslau, Brünn, Brüssel, Cassel, Cölln, Coburg, Copenhagen, Constanz Dessau, Dresden, Edenburg, Erlang, Frankfurt, Freyburgl, Gera, Gotha, Göttingen, Graz, Halle, Hamburg, Hannover, Heidelburg, Hermanstadt, Kaschau, Klagenfurt, Königraz, Königsberg, Laybach, Leiden, Leipzig, Lemberg, Linz, Lübeck, Lüttich, Magdeburg, Maynz, Mastheim [Mannheim?], München, Münster, Nürnberg, Passau, Pest und Osen, Petersburg, Prague, Preßburg, Regensburg, Riga, Salzburg, Stuttgard, Strasburg, Speyr, Stockholm, Troppau, Tübingen, Ulm, Warschau, Weimar, Wien, Wienerisch Neustadt, Würzburg, Winterthur, and Zürich.[36]

This long list is provided in its entirety to demonstrate not only the extent of its coverage, but also the inclusion of small towns along with major cities.

Another way for music to migrate, perhaps even the most important, was from publisher to publisher. The evidence that has surfaced thus far suggests that this was a well-developed means of transmission and one that has, at present, received little attention. Publishers in business with one another arranged for the reciprocal sale of publications, exchanged plates, and exchanged each others' engravings, to which they added their own title pages. Artaria, for example, issued music in London through the firm of Longman and Broderip. André had exchange arrangements with Götz, Simrock, Schott and Hummel, among others, and he printed music of other publishers. Perhaps he had arrangements with them, as well.[37] Correspondence between Pleyel and other firms has received some attention; it illustrates the nature of transactions between publishing firms.

Thus J.J. Hummel in Amsterdam writes to Pleyel in 1800 concerning a publishing project he believes would be more feasible for Pleyel's French firm:

> In addition I have a question to ask you, Monsieur. It is that if you are or would be intending to print J. Haydn's oratorio *Die Schöpfung*, then I would like to make you a proposition. In fact, I have it in preparation and to tell the truth, it is too large a work for me, and I wish I had not undertaken it. Since this sort of thing is more customary in France, where large scores are printed, I think it would be better for your house. I would prefer to issue it not in score, but in separate parts. If you are inclined to do it, then I shall let you have what is necessary for it, with the plates, for the same that it cost me, and then you finish it up and I take a number of copies from you for it. I think this would be something for you, since you can bring it to completion in Paris more easily and sooner.[38]

A collection of letters between Pleyel and Hoffmeister & Co. provides a detailed view of their business transactions, which may even be typical. Many of the letters describe exchanges of music and the necessary financial arrangements. Pleyel writes, in a letter to Hoffmeister: "In short I do all I can to satisfy you. A crate of music will shortly arrive in Hamburg which contains four to six copies of almost everything in my catalogue; this is intended for you."[39] A later letter from Pleyel asks for 50 copies of everything and also addresses the question of rights in France:

> It is really very difficult for me to print the name of your firm on works that are already printed; but on the works which I shall engrave in the future I shall have it placed as you request; similarly you should place my address and the words 'enregistré à la Bibliothèque nationale' on those works of yours of which you wish the *propriété* in France, and I will take two copies at once to the Bibliothèque so that no one may pirate them. Send me as soon as you can 50 copies of all your new issues.[40]

In a letter from November 1800, Pleyel asks Hoffmeister to pick up anything new and interesting in Vienna that might be worth printing:

> Go at once to Vienna and send me all the sonatas by Pethofen [Beethoven] except the trios for piano, 3 sonatas dedicated to

Haydn and 2 sonatas with violoncello; these are already engraved by me. If you find something by Kozeluk or anything else that is good and worth engraving, send it to me by the mail coach to Frankfurt care of Geil & Hädler, music merchants.[41]

Pleyel's proposal to Hoffmeister for their continued course of business is worth quoting at length, since it describes in some detail the nature of transactions that could have taken place between many of the major firms:

> First plan: I turn over to H. Hofmeister and Kühnel as many copies as they wish of my whole catalogue at fifty percent commission, to which I contribute five percent of the shipping costs; exceptions to these are all works issued by subscription, for which I can only give 25% and 5% transport costs. These latter works include the collection of quartets and the Bibliothèque Musicale of Haydn's and Mozart's collections for violin–Mozart's and Haydn's collections for the piano go for the usual price if they are on ordinary paper. For this I ask for a statement every six months, and for everything that is sold or sent H. Hofmeister and Kühnel give me a promissory note payable in three months: so that every six months our accounts are in exact order. Moreover, I accept in parallel arrangement Hofmeister's and Kühnel's catalogue for commission in France under the same terms; but H. Hofmiester and Kühnel must defray the expenses of the customs or customs' house, for otherwise I cannot pass on their music to my agents since I must give them fifty percent. That would be, more or less, the first plan. The second is better and more profitable for both parties, but it does require a capital outlay of 50,000 livres. Second plan: I am willing to establish a principal warehouse in Germany, either in Frankfurt or another town, from which all other warehouses, music-shops and book-sellers can be furnished at 30 to 50% discount.[42]

Though the Pleyel-Hoffmeister correspondence is from the turn of the century, we know that publishers interacted earlier; their transactions may well be typical of those that had been taking place for decades. Our knowledge of business dealings between other publishers is incomplete, but further investigation might yield similar results. Bremner imported music from Hummel during the 1760's (see p. 28 above) and Westphal must have had dealings with many publishers. It would be worth investigating the details of their arrangements. A 1779 letter from Breitkopf to Artaria describes a possible formal business arrangement between them (in fact this is nearly the earliest point at which such letter could have been written to Artaria, as they did not establish their own printing outfit until 1778).

> As far as the discount is concerned, I can give you 25 percent from what I have printed at my own music publishing firm, but no more than 12 percent from foreign printed editions. From my firm I could also give more, if you are accustomed to giving more from your own, and it would end up the same–what one of us would offer the other would have to offer as well. But as for foreign items, like those sent to you now, it must remain at 12 percent. Above all I would like to have your catalogue with prices, which you send to me either by the post if it is not too heavy, or through local friends of mine: the booksellers Gräffer, Kraus, van Ghelen, Bernardi, Weingand or Hr. Thomann.... I also have a sizable business in hand-copied music, of which most is neither printed nor engraved. Of them I have published a catalogue with a theme printed for each.[43]

* * * * * * * * * * * * * * * *

These examples of international trading and connections between publishers (and many others "too tedious to mention") support a view of the eighteenth-century music trade as having been much more well-established and internationally based than has been traditionally believed. Acceptance of such a view calls into question some of the commonly-held beliefs about the distribution of music at this time, particularly the nature of piracy, multiple publication of a given work, and the isolation of places like Vienna from the trade.

The word "piracy" frequently appears in both contemporary and modern descriptions of music transmission of this time. It existed, certainly; nevertheless, many cases should be investigated more thoroughly as to whether they represented true piracy (or theft), as opposed to legitimate trade arrangements. The traditional view is that "piracy" was rampant throughout Europe during the eighteenth century; it has been suggested more often than any other as the explanation for otherwise undocumented transmission of music.[44] To be sure, there are enough well-documented examples of prints known to be unauthorized, references such as those in the Mozart correspondence to unscrupulous copyists, and citations like the following from an announcement for the début of Pleyel's publishing firm to convince us that piracy was a real threat:

No copies will be issued without Pleyel's signature; this blanket rule is necessary not so much for the publisher's interest, as for music dealers and amateurs, who for some years and especially in the last months have been shamefully deceived by pirating printers, who sell under the name of Pleyel many works which are supposed to be by this author and, when many of them were shown him in Paris, he did not recognize them and explained they were false and not his compositions.[45]

Breitkopf alludes to piracy and the problem of false attributions in the "Nacherinnerung" to the first part of his catalogue. Nevertheless, piracy is perhaps given too quickly as an explanation for undocumented transmission of a work, especially since other possible avenues have not yet been explored, particularly those of foreign distribution of a work by agents and other publishers, both working closely and in agreement with the original publisher.

Furthermore, the modern sense of piracy may be somewhat anachronistic when used to describe practices that were common during the eighteenth century. Possible occurrences of piracy are most often explained as having been due to "unscrupulous copyists." But it may not have been a question of ethics. Inextricably linked with the modern concept of piracy is the development of international copyright law, as well as the related notion of intellectual property; neither was really in place until the later part of the eighteenth century into the nineteenth.[46] In most cases reprinting of a musical work without the composer's sanction simply was not an illegal activity until very late in the eighteenth century.[47] Composers most often received a one-time sum from the initial sale of a manuscript to a publisher and retained no further interest in the work; thereafter, publishers were more concerned with each other than with the composer.[48]

The commonplace idea that many parts of Europe were isolated from the flourishing trade needs to be questioned. The seemingly remote corners and small towns represented alongside major centers in sources like the *Almanach de la librairie* should help to dispel this idea. In Vienna, for example, while it is true that the local music printing industry did not become active until 1778 when Artaria first started engraving his own prints, this relatively late starting date may have been due not merely to Vienna's geographic isolation, but also to a host of other factors which have not been adequately investigated. It seems likely that the importation of foreign prints into Vienna both before and after ca. 1780 has been underestimated. Both Artaria and Torricella, the first Viennese music printing houses, started in business by importing prints; Artaria and perhaps the others as well continued this practice even after they started engraving their own. Many examples exist from the last decades of the eighteenth century of publishing arrangements between resident composers and foreign publishers; these copies often circulated in Vienna. Krommer's Op. 13 flute quartet was published by André in 1798–it was this print that was offered in the 1799 Traeg catalogue–and was also published in Vienna, by Cappi (PN 998), in about 1807. This practice may very well have carried on earlier. What *is* established about the earlier period is that many works of Viennese composers were printed elsewhere, whatever the composer's level of involvement. For example, Vanhal's Op. 7 flute quartets were published in Paris in 1771 and advertised in the 1772 Breitkopf catalogue. They were later published in Amsterdam by Hummel, and in London by Welcker, W. Napier, and A. Hamilton. The 1799 Traeg catalogue includes these quartets, so they must have been available in Vienna; we do not know how early Traeg possessed them and if he had one of the foreign prints.

The state of the Viennese book trade must have affected the music trade. Until the 1780s strict censorship was in effect, severely limiting the books that could be printed. In 1776 J.G. Krünitz speculated whether the newly formed *Hannauer neuer Bücher-Umschlag* would "bring system and order into the Austrian book trade which has been in decay for the past 20 years."[49] Vienna did not have the well-established engraving tradition that Paris had and therefore, not as many qualified engravers. According to Johann Pezzl, writing in 1788: "In general, books printed in Vienna lack beauty and are neither well designed nor free of errors." After citing new typefaces in use by some of the local printers that are "as attractive as any used abroad," Pezzl hypothesizes that "a corresponding improvement in the quality of paper and printing ink would soon raise standards to the level of those found elsewhere." About the printing trade:

> Forty years ago this activity was a monopoly of the Jesuits. Later, newly established printers were poorly equipped and their production consisted largely of prayer-books, school books, legal documents and news sheets and paper was of poor quality. In 1781 the general publication of pamphlets was permitted and many printers came into existence, with the result that there are now twenty publishers in Vienna with about 118 presses at work.[50]

After all, Artaria and Torricella, among the first engravers to publish music exclusively in Vienna, were both foreigners. Until late in the century it was doubtless more profitable and even preferable for composers to send their works elsewhere to be engraved. The music printing industries in Paris and

London were more highly developed, and they welcomed music of foreign composers.

It is important to keep in mind that our views of eighteenth-century music publishing in Vienna derive almost exclusively from the single example of Joseph Haydn–and his practices may well have been everything other than typical. Although his music was widely disseminated throughout Europe as early as the 1760s, we do not possess much evidence of any direct relation between him and any publishers during this time. For this reason, these earlier prints are considered "inauthentic" by Haydn scholars. In addition, he is credited with the "invention" in the 1780s of the soon-to-be common practice of insuring simultaneous publication of a work in different countries. The multitude of "inauthentic" prints, especially those from before the 1780s, have not been systematically examined for what they reveal about dissemination.

Indeed, it seems plausible that Haydn's works, along with works of other successful composers, might have been traded back and forth between publishers. Haydn's Op. 1 Quartets were his first works to be printed, by Chevardière in 1764, by Hummel in 1765 and by Bremner, also in 1765.[51] We do not know how Chevardiere came to have possession of these works. The Op. 33 Quartets and the other works of the early 1780s heralded the beginning of a new era for Haydn; released from the constraints of his previous contract, at Esterhazy, he was free to play a greater role in seeing to the publication of his music.[52] Much has been made of Op. 33's wide dissemination due to its immediate success and popularity. But his earlier quartets were also disseminated widely soon after the first publication, indeed soon after their composition, regardless of the role that Haydn did or did not play. Op. 9 (c.1769–70) was published in London by Longman, Lukey in 1771, by Hummel in Amsterdam ca. 1771 and in Paris by Huberty in 1772. Op. 17 (1771) was published in 1772 in London by Longman and Broderip, as well as by Gardom and Hummel in Amsterdam. Sieber in Paris published them the next year and Welcker in London in 1775. Subsequent publishers included Imbault, Pleyel and Schott.

The view of a music publishing world as a well-connected network of dealers exchanging music, perhaps even entire contents of their catalogues, sheds new light on the question of publication of a given work by several publishers in close succession. Haydn's wide international distribution of his music has been explained by the mere fact of his fame and reputation. Yet if publishers regularly exchanged their stock, multiple publication and wide dissemination of works by other composers must also have been common. For example, Carl Stamitz privately published his Op. 13 symphonies in London in 1777.[53] They were published almost simultaneously by Hummel in Amsterdam and Sieber in Paris. Stamitz's involvement in the first printing might suggest that he had his own business arrangement with Hummel and Sieber. J.C. Bach's Op. 17 keyboard sonatas were published within about five or six years (ca. 1774–80) by John Welcker in London, Hummel in Amsterdam, Sieber in Paris, André in Offenbach, and Huberty in Vienna.[54] There are many similar examples from the eighteenth century of works published in close succession by several publishers, many of which might be explained by business relationships between the publishers involved rather than by "piracy."

This survey touches on only a few of the many issues that deserve examination; some of the conclusions remain in part conjectural. Collecting the evidence continues to resemble assembly of a jig-saw puzzle, yet each new fact fits cleanly into the overall picture of an international publishing world based on close collaboration, one with many similarities to today's practices. As we continue to unearth information about the business aspects of music, many of these conjectures may well be verified. Study of international distribution of music via publishers may even be crucial to an understanding of the development of musical style and influence.

Endnotes

1   Hans Lenneberg has done important work on the subject of music dissemination: "Music Publishing and Dissemination in the Early Nineteenth Century," *The Journal of Musicology* 2 (1983):174–84; and "Early Circulating Libraries and the Dissemination of Music," *The Library Quarterly* 52 (1982):122–30. The recent guide edited by D.W. Krummel and Stanley Sadie, *Music Printing and Publishing* (New York: W.W. Norton & Co., 1990) is a significant contribution. As for individual publishers, more work has been done on those from Paris than anywhere else. Some of this includes: Rita Benton with Jeanne Halley, *Pleyel as Music Publisher* (Stuyvesant, NY: Pendragon, 1989); Anik Devriès, *Édition et commerce de la musique gravée à Paris dans la première moitié du XVIIIe siècle* (Geneva: Editions Minkoff, 1976); Anik Devriès and François Lesure, *Dictionnaire des éditeurs de musique français*, 2 vols (Geneva: Minkoff, 1979 & 1988): Cari Johansson, *French Music Publishers' Catalogues of the Second Half of the Eighteenth Century* (Stockholm: Kungl. Musikverleger Akademia Bibliotek, 1958). Monographs on German publishers include: Hans Schneider, *Der Musikverleger Johann Michael Götz* (Tutzing: Hans Schneider, 1989); Wolfgang Matthäus, *Johann André: Musikverlag zu Offenbach am Main* (Tutzing: Hans Schnelder, 1973); and Alexander Weinmann's work on Viennese publishers. For England there is only Charles Humphries and William C. Smith, *Music Publishing in the British Isles*, 2nd ed. (New York: Barnes & Noble, 1970).

2   Joel Sachs, "Authentic English and French Editions of J.N. Hummel," *Journal of the American Musicological Society* 25 (1972): 203–4, 209.

3   One such description may be found in Alec Hyatt King, "General Musical Conditions," in Gerald Abraham, ed., *The Age of Beethoven 1790–1830*, vol. 8 of *The New Oxford History of Music* (Oxford: Oxford University Press 1982) 2.

4   "The Commerce of Letters: The Study of the Eighteenth-Century Book Trade," *Eighteenth Century Studies* 17 (1983–1984): 409.

5   Barry Brook's investigation of the symphonie concertante. *La Symphonie Française dans la seconde moitié du XVIIIe siècle* (Paris: Publications de l'Institut de Musicologie, 1962), while ground-breaking for its time, was limited to France.

6   This research serves as background for my dissertation for Cornell University, "Quartets and Quintets for Mixed Groups of Winds and Strings in Vienna: Mozart and his Contemporaries in Vienna, c. 1780–c.1800."

7   See Rita Benton, *Ignace Pleyel: A Thematic Catalogue of His Compositions* (New York: Pendragon, 1977). In addition to André, they were offered by Artaria, Boyer, Hummel, Longman, and Schott in 1789: Imbault in 1791–2; Sieber in 1799; Broderip and Preston in c. 1800: Cappi in 1807; even as late as 1841–5 by Ewer. These three quartets were also arranged and published for string quartet, clarinet quartet, various trio versions, duo version, solo, orchestral, vocal, etc.

8   See Antoine Perrin, *Almanach de la librairie* (1781; reprint, Aubel: P.M. Gason, 1984); and also Giles Barber, "Pendred Abroad," in *Studies in the Book Trade in Honour of Graham Pollard* (Oxford: Oxford Bibliographical Society, 1975).

9   Cliff Eisen, *New Mozart Documents* (Stanford: Stanford University Press, 1991): 37.

10 Barry Brook, "The Symphonie Concertante: An Interim Report," *The Musical Quarterly* 47 (1961): 494.

11 Anik Devriès, *Édition et commerce*, 82.

12 Emily Anderson, ed., *Letters of Mozart and His Family,* 2nd ed. (London: Macmillan & Co, 1966), 2: 591.

13 Ibid., 2:592.

14 Ibid., 2:737.

15 Quoted from Brook, *La Symphonie Française*, 37.

16 *Journal de musique* (Paris, 1770; reprint. Geneva: Minkoff, 1972) 10. "Pour remplir cet objet dans toute son étendue, nous nous sommes ouvert de correspondances dans l'Italie, l'Espagne, l'Allemagne et l'Angleterre. Nous osons donc espérer que ce Journal sera bien reçu de tous les Pays." I have preserved original spellings of place and proper names in quotations from eighteenth-century sources, giving modern spellings in square brackets only when the original seems unclear. The translations are my own and originals are provided when from a primary source.

17 *Calendrier musical universel* (Paris, 1788–89; reprint Geneva: Minkoff, 1972), [i]. "la notice des pièces en musique représentées à Paris, à Versailles, à Saint-Cloud, sur les differens Théatres de l'Europe, tels que ceux de Londres, de Vienne, de Saint Pétersbourg, et des principals villes d'Italie."

18 *Journal de musique* (Paris, 1777; reprint, Geneva: Minkoff, 1972), 2151–52. "On croit donc rendre service aux amateurs & leur donner une nouvelle intéressante en annonçant qu'on a formé au Bureau du *Journal de musique*, rue Montmartre, vis-à-vis celle des Vieux Augustins, une collection précieuse de partitions italiennes & de plus

de 400 ariettes nouvelles de meilleurs maîtres, tels qu'Anfossi, Piccini, Maïo, Sacchini, Paisiello & c. & c. On pourra s'en procurer des copies au prix ordinaire, & pour peu que cette annonce ait de succès, on continuera d'y faire venir les opéra nouveaux qui seront les plus applaudis sur les différens théâtres d'Italie et former ainsi une sorte de bibliotheque d'un genre unique composée de tout ce qu'il y a de meilleur dans la musique étrangere, qu'on s'empressera de communiquer à tous ceux qui le desiront. Le prix de ces copies est fixé à 4 f. la page."

19   *Almanach musical* (Paris, 1775; reprint, Geneva: Minkoff, 1972), 147. "Les éditeurs sont ceux qui ont fait graver des ouvrages de musique et qui ne tiennent chez eux que la musique de leur fonts. Les marchands sont ceux qui ne se bornent pas à la musique de leur fonts et tiennent un magasin assorti de celle des Auteurs, des Editeurs et des Autres marchand."

20   Anik Devriès, *Édition et commerce*, 18. "toutes sortes de belles musiques, tant françaises, latines d'impression et de gravures qu'italiennes & autres des meilleurs auteurs: de gravures d'Hollande et qu'il les donnera au meilleur marché qu'il se puisse & presque au prix coûtant."

21   Ibid., 43. "Catalogue général de musique imprimée ou gravée en France. Ensemble de celle qui est imprimée dans les pays étrangers dont on fait usage. 1734. Se vend à Paris, chez le Sieur Leclerc."

22   Quoted in François Lesure, *Bibliographie des éditions musicales publiées par Estienne Roger et Michel-Charles Le Céne* (Paris: Société Française de Musicologie, 1969) 21.

23   Cari Johansson, *French Music Publishers' Catalogues*, 86, n. 10.

24   David Wyn Jones, "Haydn's Music in London in the Period 1760–1790," *Haydn Yearbook* 14 (1983): 153.

25   See Wyn Jones, "Haydn's Music in London." Wyn Jones's information goes beyond that in either Hoboken or *Joseph Haydn Werke*. Bremner apparently added his own title page to Hummel's edition.

26   Other obvious choices of figures to follow up include Christian Gottfried Thomas of Leipzig, Johann Karl Rellstab of Berlin, and Laurenz Lausch of Vienna. Lending libraries may have played an important role in the dissemination of music. See Hans Lenneberg, "Early Circulating Libraries," and A.H. King, "Music Circulating Libraries in Britain," *Musical Times* 119/120 (1978): 134–8.

27   See Klaus Hortschansky, "Zwei datierte Hummel-Kataloge" in Kurt Dorfmüller, ed., *Quellenstudien zur Musik* (Frankfurt: C.F. Peters, 1972), 91–92.

28   Quoted in H.C. Robbins Landon, *Haydn: Chronicle and Works* (Bloomington: Indiana University Press, 1976), 3:27–28. The original is now in the Burgenländisches Landesmuseum at Eisenstadt.

29   Quoted in Eisen, *New Mozart Documents*, 54.

30   Miriam Terry, "C.P.E. Bach and Westphal: A Clarification," *Journal of the American Musicological Society* 22 (1969): 108.

31   This notice appeared on the catalogue that was attached to "Six Sonatas for the Violoncello composed by L. Boccherini," (M231 B66 1780z). It most likely dates from the 1780s.

32   See Johansson, *J.J. & B. Hummel Music-Publishing*, 6.

33 See Ibid., F.1 and F.8, respectively. "On trouve chez le même des Catalogues gratis de Plusieurs Musiques Etrangères, Imprimé à Paris, Londres et en Allemagnes." "Ce Catalogue se distribue gratis chez le susdit & les Correspondants."

34 *Musikalische Realzeitung*, ed. Heinrich Philipp Carl Bossler (Speyer, 1788–1790; reprint Hildesheim & New York: George Olms, 1971), 3. "Herr cantor Bißmann und Kompagnie in Frankfurt am Main verkaufen nebst den in Kommission habenden Musikalien des Berliner, Mannheimer, Speierschen, Offenbacher und andern Verlags auch ächte romanische Violinsaiten. . ."

35 Matthäus, *Johann André*, 56–57.

36 Quoted in Eisen, *New Mozart Documents*, 37.

37 Matthäus, *Johann André*, 43–51.

38 Quoted in Rita Benton, "Pleyel as Music Publisher," *Journal of the American Musicological Society*, 32 (1979): 132. Pleyel apparently took Hummel up on a offer and published *Die Schöpfung* in 1801. PN 359 (RISM H25251).

39 Quoted in Else Radant, "Ignaz Pleyel's Correspondence with Hoffmeister & Co.," *Haydn Yearbook* 12 (1981): 141.

40 Quoted in Ibid., 147.

41 Quoted in Ibid., 148.

42 Quoted in Ibid., 161–62.

43 Letter from 30 October, 1779 quoted in Rosemary Hilmar, *Der Musikverlag Artaria & Comp.* (Tutzing, 1977). 13–14. "Was nun den Rabat anbelangt, so kann ich Ihnen von meinem eigenen musikalischen Verlage, was ich gedruckt habe, 25. pCt. von fremden gedruckten Musikalien aber nicht wohl mehr als 12 pCt. geben. Von meinem Verlage könnte [ich] auch wohl mehr geben, wenn Sie gewohnt sind vom Ihrigen mehr zu geben, und es würde dann auf eines herauskommen, was einer giebt, würde der andere Theil auch thun müßen. Beym fremden Sachen aber, als wie die itzt Ihnen überchickten Sachen, muß es bey 12 pCt. bleiben. . . Vor allen Dingen wünschte ich wohl ihren Catal. mit Preisen zu haben, den Sie mir entweder wenn er nicht so stark ist, mit der Post oder durch einem der dortigen Freunde von mir/als Hr. Buchhändler Gräffer, Kraus, van Ghelen, Bernardi, Weingand oder Hr. Thomann/übersenden.... Ich habe auch einen starken Verkehr mit geschrieben Musicalien, wovon die meisten weder gedruckt, noch gestochen sind. Davon habe ich einen Catalog herausgegeben, wo von jedem Stücke die Themata gedruckt sind."

44 See Barry Brook "Piracy and Panacea," *R.M.A. Proceedings* 102 (1975–76): 13–36.

45 Quoted in Benton, "Pleyel as Music Publisher," 128.

46 See Martha Woodmansee, "The Genius and the Copyright: Economic and Legal Conditions of the Emergence of the Author," *Eighteenth Century Studies* 17 (1983–84): 425-48.

47 David Hunter, "Music Copyright in Britain to 1800," *Music and Letters* 67/3 (1986): 272.

48 *Ibid.*, 271.

49 Quoted in Giles Barber, "Pendred Abroad" in *Studies in the Book Trade in Honour of Graham Pollard* (Oxford: Oxford Bibliographical Society, 1975): 275.

50 Quoted in H. C. Robbins Landon, *Mozart and Vienna* (New York: Schirmer, 1991), 173–74.

51 *Josef Haydn Werke*, Kritischer Bericht, Reihe XII Band 1, Frühe Streichquartette, ed., George Feder, (München: G. Henle Verlag, 1973), 25–26.

52   James Webster, "Prospects for Haydn Biography after Landon," *The Musical Quarterly* 68 (1982): 490.

53   See Jenny Pickering, "Printing, Publishing and the Migration of Sources: The Case of Carl Stamitz," *Brio* 27/2 (Autumn/Winter 1990): 59–66.

54   See *Collected Works of J.C. Bach*, ed. Stephen Roe, 42, Keyboard Music (New York: Garland, 1989), xi; and Matthäus, *Johann André*, 116.

Venetian Printed Anthologies of Music in the 1560s and the Role of the Editor *

GIULIO M. ONGARO

The third quarter of the sixteenth century was a time of change for the Venetian music printing business, particularly the decade that ended with the deaths of its two most important figures, Antonio Gardano in 1569, and Girolamo Scotto in 1572. These changes were perhaps not as dramatic as the introduction of single impression printing to Venice earlier in the century, but they are indicative of a long transition. One sign of this transition is a different approach on the part of Venetian publishers to the publication of anthologies, especially visible in a growing number of collections sharing some particular traits, which, for lack of a better term, we could call "real" anthologies. In the course of the present article I will define this term in more detail; first, however, I propose to tackle the problem of establishing a taxonomy for musical anthologies, thus providing a basis for the discussion of those changes that I see occurring in the third quarter of the century. After this discussion, I will identify some of those individuals who were instrumental in introducing changes to Venetian music publishing in the 1560s, examining in particular the career of one Giulio Bonagiunta da San Genesi, editor of several musical collections.

When we think about musical anthologies, the fact that not all are conceptually identical ought to be evident; nevertheless, in a characteristically insightful aside, Lorenzo Bianconi has observed that scholars studying sixteenth-century printed anthologies of music often have not discriminated among rather different models. He identifies two of these models, the "florilegio," an anthology compiled from previously published pieces, and the "edizione collettiva," an anthology of pieces composed conceptually as a unit, perhaps following a pre-determined plan, which might be (but most often is not) a musical one.[1] Regarding this subject, James Haar also has commented on the appearance in the late 1560s of retrospective collections of the "florilegio" type, which in his opinion show a new and different historical consciousness, citing as an example *La eletta di tutta la musica intitolata Corona* published in Venice by Zuan Jacomo Zorzi,[2] which consists of proven winners, of pieces already circulating in print, a

43

practice which appears in music published outside Venice a few decades earlier.[3] What Bianconi did not say–probably because it is so obvious–but I would like to add for completeness' sake, is that there are at least two more categories of musical anthologies which were present since the inception of music printing. The first of these categories is the pseudo-anthology, that is an anthology recognized as such for bibliographic purposes, but that in practice is a single-composer print with few (often one) additions by others,[4] while the other type is the anthology compiled from pieces not previously published, but gathered without a manifest plan, perhaps only depending on the availability of the repertory or according to genre considerations (it will suffice to think of the various *Madrigali a tre voci, Madrigali di diversi*, etc.). We can better understand the differences among these types of anthologies, the processes involved in collecting them and bringing them to press, and their intended function if we refer to what must have been to sixteenth-century Venetian publishers a very obvious model, that is the Italian lyric poetry anthology. As a phenomenon, poetic anthologies share many (though not all) characteristics of musical anthologies, but appear on the scene earlier, because of the technical problems that had to be solved to print polyphonic music and because the rather specialized music market might not have seemed very promising to the early pioneers of this new medium. One noticeable difference between these two genres is that Italian prints of poetry were at first largely retrospective in character, because the established canon was that of the fourteenth century, a situation without parallel in music at the beginning of music printing, when both the testimony of contemporary writers and the evidence of the prints show the focus to have been on more recent material, no more than a generation old.[5] The retrospective quality of musical prints such as *La eletta di tutta la musica*, is slight by comparison with earlier poetic anthologies, extending in fact only to the rather recent past. In this sense its direct parallel is the *Fiori delle rime de' poeti illustri*, edited by Girolamo Ruscelli in 1558, which represents the first summary of Petrarchan (or rather Bembist) poetry.[6] Aside from questions of precedence and chronology, some to be discussed later, it is undeniable that the same sub-genres exist both in musical and poetic anthologies produced by the Venetian presses in the sixteenth century.[7] Thus, the appearance of the "edizione collettiva" anthology, and particularly of the celebratory "edizione collettiva," first in poetry collections and later in music,[8] is evidence of another conceptual framework, one where instead of using an anthology merely as repository of currently available music, or as a slightly retrospective summary, the compiler displays a new attitude towards the future. This is certainly true for the several sixteenth-century poetic anthologies with titles such as "Tempio,"[9] a word that conveys images, among others, of continuity, of permanence, since one does not build a sacred edifice with the expectation that it will be tumbling down in a few years, and it is also true of their musical counterparts. The inherent ephemeral quality of a paper object, not the best building material for a lasting temple, is overcome by the sheer number of copies available.

Although the publication of musical anthologies was not a new phenomenon in the 1560s, Venetian publishers changed their output in this decade by producing an increasing number of mostly secular anthologies not dominated by a single composer, sometimes compiled around a single literary theme, and supplied with a catchy title, undoubtedly (to use a modern term) for marketing reasons: this is precisely the type I have called the "real" anthology. Each of these anthologies might be a "florilegio" or "edizione collettiva," or an anthology assembled without a definite plan, but what they have in common, in my opinion, is the different conceptual approach evidenced by the title. While it is obvious that any title page serves as an advertisement for the contents of the print, I am concerned here with titles whose link to the contents is either tenuous at best, or based purely on literary (non-musical) or commercial considerations.[10] For this reason, I would not include in this group titles of anthologies which advertise genres (e.g. *Canzoni sonetti strambotti e frottole libro quarto*),[11] but only titles, such as *Il lauro secco, I dolci frutti, Il desiderio, Il gaudio, Le vive fiamme*,[12] or perhaps titles that advertise groups of composers (e.g. *Musica de' virtuosi della florida capella dell' ... S. Duca di Baviera*,[13] whose commercial potential is obvious). If we compare the production of the 1550s with that of the 1560s we notice that only eleven collections fitting my criteria were published in Venice in the 1550s, and that in fact nine of the eleven collections were divided between two titles.[14] During the 1560s, on the other hand, the Venetian presses produced over thirty collections of this type, and, with the possible exception of the several *Libri delle Muse* (about a fourth of the total), no other title monopolizes this group. That this marketing practice was successful is proven by the fact that by the late 1570s and 1580s the majority of Venetian secular anthologies sported titles meant to pique the curiosity of the public.[15]

I don't know whether, as Haar suggests,[16] these trends indicate that beginning in the 1560s consumers needed to be stimulated to go on buying madrigal prints, but surely we can see a changed attitude. This is perhaps a sign that the old vestiges of musical manuscript culture were being replaced in Venice by a true industrial print culture that discovered a different marketing strategy based on creating an incentive for the consumer to buy more than he or she was otherwise inclined. Even a music lover who already owned many (or most) of the pieces included in *La eletta di tutta la musica* might have been induced to purchase the anthology of "greatest hits," through a procedure that is familiar to us, experienced consumers that we are, but whose potential I am not sure had been immediately grasped by sixteenth-century producers. I remind you also that while a title such as *Madrigali di diversi*, or *Canzoni sonetti strambotti e frottole* is similar to one that might be penned on the outer folio of a manuscript collection, the same cannot be said of *Il gaudio*, or *Le vive fiamme*.[17] The new, modern attitudes of the Venetian printing press in the 1560s are reflected also in the establishment of a guild for booksellers and printers. Although the Venetian government had prepared legislation regulating the publishing business as early as 1549, the statutes were not implemented until 1566, and by-laws were approved a year later in 1567.[18]

In the case of musical anthologies, there is little question that Girolamo Scotto should be considered one of the most influential figures in the transition to new models. Of the thirty-six "real" anthologies printed in Venice between 1560 and 1569, twenty-two were published by Scotto, while Gardano published only nine; the rest are distributed among Rampazetto, Merulo and Zorzi (and I should add that Rampazetto is known to have had occasional joint ventures with Scotto).[19] The division of the eleven collections from the 1550s had been virtually even: six for Scotto and five for Gardano. As you can see, Gardano's output in this "genre" remained almost constant, while Scotto's increased dramatically. One of the possible reasons for Scotto's exploration of this type of anthology might be that he was, on the whole, not as dependent as his rival Gardano on the success of his publishing ventures and thus was able to essay new projects without putting his whole business at risk. It is noteworthy that the printer most responsible for the establishment of printed anthologies of lyric poetry, Gabriel Giolito, was in a similar financial situation, and that some have seen in his business behavior the signs of an "intense mercantile drive," similar to what Scotto might have acquired in his non-musical business ventures.[20]

The 1560s were also a time when some musicians employed by the church of St. Mark's seriously attempted to break into the music publishing business, either as editors working for established publishers, or even, as did Claudio Merulo, by launching an independent printing press. It would not be accurate to say that musicians in Venice had been totally absent from the publishing business before the 1560s: the example of Willaert's 1536 arrangements of Verdelot's madrigals for lute and voice represents a commercial enterprise, if there ever was one, and lesser figures were also involved, although not always as music printers.[21] On the other hand, it is obvious that the role of musicians in the Venetian printing trade is more visible beginning in the 1560s, perhaps reflecting a perception on their part that opportunities for financial gain were to be found there.[22]

GIULIO BONAGIUNTA DA SAN GENESI

In the mid-1560s an obscure singer and composer, Giulio Bonagiunta da San Genesi, entered the Venetian publishing world, becoming the most prolific editor of the period: from 1565 to 1568 Bonagiunta's name is on at least eleven madrigal prints (mostly anthologies), three prints of *napolitane*, three books of motets, and a book of Lasso masses. There is evidence that his publishing activities were known and appreciated both within the relatively small circle of Venetian musicians and elsewhere. For instance in 1568 the composer Baldassare Donato, a lifelong member (and later *maestro*) of the chapel of St. Mark's and *maestro* of its *cappella piccola* from 1562 to 1565, declared in the dedication of his second book of four-voice madrigals that in preparing the collection from madrigals he had saved over a period of time, he had "conferred with Messer Giulio Bonagiunta singer of St. Mark's, about [his] intention."[23] Apparently, then, Bonagiunta was sufficiently respected as an editor to be consulted by one of his superiors in the hierarchy of the ducal chapel and to warrant the appearance of his name on title pages with a frequency rarely matched by other music editors. His professional career as editor is patterned after those of the great editors of non-musical publications active in sixteenth-century Venetian printing circles. One case particularly relevant to Bonagiunta's career is that of Lodovico Dolce, who, beginning earlier in the century, edited a number of volumes of prose and poetry working almost exclusively for Gabriele Giolito de' Ferrari.[24]

Before examining further Bonagiunta's activities as editor, however, I would like to provide some small additions to the available biographical information.[25] A relative wealth of information is available on Bonagiunta for the years from 1560 to 1568, while virtually nothing is known about the remainder of his life. In all the dedications and title pages he calls himself "da San Genesi." There are at least two S. Genesi or S. Ginesio in Italy, one in the Marche region, located near Macerata, the other, traditionally indicated as Bonagiunta's birthplace, near Pavia, in Lombardy.[26] The dedications of Bonagiunta's anthologies (always signed by him) do not always offer biographical information, but two of them are helpful in confirming our Giulio as being instead from San Ginesio near Macerata. The first one comes from the 1568 madrigal print *Corona della morte dell'illustre signor ... Annibal Caro* (RISM 1568[16]), published by

Scotto and dedicated to Giovanni Ferro da Macerata. Bonagiunta writes:

> "...I think I would deserve not a little shame if, through my work
> I did not expand and make public the praises of my fellow coun-
> trymen [compatrioti] in any way I can, just as they have brought
> honor and glory to our country [la sua & mia patria] with their
> accomplishments."[27]

It is not clear whether he is referring to Caro or Ferro in this sentence, but he might refer to either one or both, since Caro was a native of Civitanova Marche and had been admitted in 1551 to the Collegio dei Cavalieri Lauretani,[28] and Ferro, himself a *Cavaliere*, was from Macerata.

The second dedication, taken from the fifth book of motets by Lasso, published by Claudio Merulo in 1568, provides final confirmation. Bona-giunta dedicated the print to Vincenzo de Lucchis, bishop of Ancona, saying: "Four years ago, when I passed through Ancona on my way home, having stopped there for three days, the musician Hector Vidue, the director of your choir, brought me to you so that I could pay you my respects."[29] Bonagiunta was certainly living in Venice between 1562 and 1565, and this bit of information makes it clear that his hometown was San Genesi near Macerata (in the territory of Ancona) and not the one in Lombardy.

The first archival documents about Bonagiunta's career come from the archives of the Santa Casa of Loreto, where he was "chierico e cantore" from December 15, 1560 to June 7, 1561 with a salary of 36 florins a year. Other documents indicate that he was made a canon of the church on April 1, 1562.[30] Bonagiunta was hired at St. Mark's on October 14, 1562. The hiring document tells us that he was a contralto and that he was to re-ceive 80 ducats a year, a salary somewhat above the average for singers of the *basilica* in that period.[31] Pannella states that Giulio had left Venice for Parma, where he was employed as musician and teacher of the *paggi*, by January 1, 1567, but this assertion is not supported by the evidence.[32] Bonagiunta stayed at St. Mark's at least until April 1568, when he was given a monetary gift for a trip to Bavaria (clearly taken for official or semi-official business).[33] Although his stay in Venice was interrupted by frequent absences, numerous documents and signed dedications confirm his presence in the city until the late spring of 1568.[34] Some of his absences were related to offers of employment elsewhere. In 1566 he was lured, to-gether with Galeazzo de Pedris da Pesaro, a bass singer at St. Mark's, by the agent of the Archduke Karl to join his chapel in Graz, but the singers, after initially accepting, changed their minds.[35] It is unclear whether the two singers actually left Venice for a time: one document seems to suggest that they headed for Bavaria and that Giulio was recalled to Venice by letters of the Procuratori.[36] Evidence of his contacts with Bavaria is particularly interesting not only because of the clear implications for his friendship with Lasso, but also in view of the fact that in Bonagiunta's anthologies one finds the names of many musicians active in Munich (and in some cases, also later in Venice), such as Francesco Bonardo, Giuseppe Guami, Ivo de Vento, whose music he could have collected on this or other trips.

Bonagiunta's absences from service at St. Mark's and other evidence also suggest that the singer must have had a somewhat impulsive personality. For instance, on 13 June 1565 he was given room and board at the monastery of Santo Stefano in Venice in exchange for performing occasionally at the services, but only four months later he had left the monastery, in spite of the fact that one of the monks was his own brother Andrea (perhaps a strong factor in his decision to come to Venice).[37] Moreover, in 1567 Bonagiunta was sentenced by a Venetian court for his role in a public altercation with another singer.[38] Given his apparent restlessness, it is possible that Bonagiunta might have accepted an appointment at the court of Parma in 1567, only to change his mind shortly afterwards, as he had done on other occasions.

What happened to Bonagiunta after 1568 is unclear: even his death date is unknown. He was apparently in Parma in late 1570, as teacher of court *paggi*, but it has not been established how long his service lasted.[39] The appearance of a 1588 Milanese print of masses by Lasso and others labelled "nunc primum a Julio Bonaiuncta editae" has led Pannella to believe that Bonagiunta was still alive at the time.[40] This volume, however, is one of a series printed in Milan that are normally reprints (sometimes expanded) of earlier publications. In the same year, for instance, the Tini publishing house reprinted another book of Lasso masses, which originally had been published by Claudio Merulo.[41] In the case of the supposed Bonagiunta print, it is also slightly suspicious that to masses by Lasso, Hawill (?=Anville) and Lhéritier (the latter surely an unusual choice for 1588) the Milanese publisher added a work by Giacomo Antonio Piccioli, *maestro di cappella* at the Duomo in Vercelli since 1587.[42] Bonagiunta probably was responsible for a missing first edition of this print, later used by the Milanese printers as a model for their anthology. It is unlikely that an editor as prolific as Bonagiunta, with his established ties to the Scotto house, could fail to produce a single print between 1568 and 1588.

There is no question that Bonagiunta was particularly interested in editing anthologies and that his model was not necessarily the only one followed by a musician active in the publishing business. Merulo, for instance, hardly printed such collections, and in its first two years of operation, his firm seems to have concentrated on prints whose cost was probably born by the composer or by a patron, and therefore financially safe.[43] In fact even some of Merulo's anthologies are reprints and do not signify a true editorial effort on his part: for instance, his *Motectarum divinitatis liber primus* (RISM 1569[2]) is a reprint of a *Mutetarum divinitatis liber primus* published in Milan by Castiglione (RISM 1543[3]). Bonagiunta, on the other hand, was so involved in the production of anthologies, that in the years 1565-1568, he edited nine out of the fifteen "real" anthologies printed in Venice.[44]

If we are to believe Bonagiunta's dedications, he was trusted and respected by no lesser composers than Rore and Lasso. In the dedication of Lasso's fifth book of motets Bonagiunta tells us: "I was given by Orlando Lasso, ... many musical compositions with the condition that I would, at my will, take care of their printing."[45] It is possible that Bonagiunta had received these compositions during Lasso's trip to Italy in 1567, when the composer visited Venice at the end of May, probably to supervise the publication of his *Libro quarto de' madrigali a cinque voci*, as we know from a letter by a merchant, Nicolò Stoppio, to Hans Jakob Fugger, dated May 25, in which Stoppio writes: "Orlando is here, and he is well, happy and a good friend to everybody; he will leave here in eight days for Ferrara with a set of madrigals that he had printed and dedicated to that Duke. We shall see how generous [the Duke] will be."[46] A short time after Lasso's visit, Bonagiunta edited the *Terzo libro del Desiderio* (dedication dated 11 June), on whose title page Lasso's name is prominently displayed, and a few weeks later the *Primo libro degli eterni mottetti di Orlando Lasso, Cipriano Rore et d'altri* (dedication dated 22 July), suggesting that he might have received some material directly from Orlando.[47] In this particular case, there is little doubt that during his Venetian sojourn Lasso was preoccupied primarily with the supervision of the printing of the collection to be presented to the Duke of Ferrara, and it should not be surprising that he would have entrusted, or sold, some of his other pieces to an editor.

Bonagiunta must have met Lasso before 1567, perhaps visiting the composer during one of his several absences from St. Mark's, in 1565.[48] In the dedication of the 1565 print *Orlandi Lassi ... quinque et sex vocibus ... sacrae cantiones* (RISM L 786), Bonagiunta writes: "since I received as a gift from Orlando Lasso, ... some songs [cantiones] called motets, which, thanks to the composer's courtesy, I was to use as I pleased, I decided to put them in print and publish them."[49] Bonagiunta also claims to have enjoyed Rore's trust, when he states in the dedication of *Le vive fiamme* (RISM

1565[18]): "thanks to the deep friendship and the loving debt which I had for a long time with the most excellent musician Cipriano Rore, he gave me, very kindly, as an act of courtesy, some of his most beautiful madrigals for four and five voices, asking me to keep them, so that his works would not fall so easily into everyone's hands."[50] Of course, one could discount Bonagiunta's claims as part of an advertising campaign; they probably contain some exaggeration, for instance on the duration of his "gran familiarità" with Rore, or on the fact that both Rore and Lasso would give him some very marketable compositions out of the goodness of their heart, but I believe that on the whole they must be taken seriously, especially considering that Bonagiunta never made similar claims for other well-known composers, such as Striggio or de Monte, whose music he edited. "Gifts" of music directly from the composer were not the only strategy used by Bonagiunta to assemble his anthologies. Other possibilities include commissioning pieces for a particular anthology,[51] or using music that Scotto might have had available in his shop. One example of the latter might be the case of Stefano Rossetto, whose *Il lamento d'Olimpia* was published by Scotto in 1567.[52] While before 1567 Rossetto's name was absent from Bonagiunta's anthologies, after that date he is represented by two settings of canzoni and a madrigal. Similarly, pieces by de Monte appear only beginning in late April 1568, and could have been acquired from the composer when he travelled from Rome to Vienna.[53]

The dedicatees of Bonagiunta's prints appear to make up a diverse group: in general it can be said that Bonagiunta does not seem to have chosen the most powerful members of the ruling class as dedicatees of his collections.[54] While prints by Lasso or de Monte–to use the example of famous composers–are usually dedicated from the composer to a ruler, a member of the ruling family, or, at least, to important court personages, Bonagiunta seems to have cultivated the lesser nobility and the wealthy bourgeoisie. Even when he dedicated his prints to Venetian patricians (e.g. Tron, Contarini, Trevisan, Grimani), the individuals selected were not the most prominent members of their families. Only one of Bonagiunta's Venetian dedicatees is clearly identifiable as a figure of more than average importance. The dedicatee of Lasso's second book of motets is Domenico Paruta, abbot of the Venetian monastery of San Gregorio; he is also the dedicatee of Andrea Gabrieli's first book of five-voice madrigals.[55] There is a fair number of dedications to gentlemen from the Venetian *terraferma*: these include Antonio Villabruna da Feltre (in the Venetian Piedmont);[56] Antonio Roncale da Rovigo whose father had been knighted by the Doge Venier in 1554; Benedetto Lazzarini, called a "Paduan gentleman;" Sigismondo Borgaso, a canon in Treviso; Giovanni Battista Bianchini and Ludovico Leggerini da Rovigo. The Rovigo connection is intriguing because Bonagiunta in dedicating his 1567 madrigal anthology *Il gaudio* to Bianchini and Leggerini seems to say that he participated in musical activities there.[57] Two of the most prominent people among the dedicatees are Vito da Dorimbergo and Ginevra Salviati de' Baglioni, foreigners residing in Venice in the 1560s. Vito da Dorimbergo was originally from the Friuli region, but was in Venice as Imperial ambassador.[58] Besides the Bonagiunta print, he was the dedicatee of the first book of four-voice madrigals of Ludovico Balbi, also a singer at St. Mark's.[59] Dorimbergo must have been active in Venetian musical circles, and his expertise was recognized: in 1569 he was asked by the Archduke Ferdinand to send some information on a Vincenzo Napolitano, described as "magister capellae" at San Giovanni dei Furlani in Venice. The Archduke must have found his reply satisfactory because he subsequently hired Vincenzo as "Hofkaplan" and tenor in 1571.[60] The other important personality to receive a dedication was Ginevra Salviati de' Baglioni: her husband Astorre Baglioni was a *capitano* in the service of the Republic, descended from a noble family of Perugia, one whose service was trusted; he achieved heroic status by being one of the Venetian defenders at the siege of Cyprus, dying there at the hands of the Turks in 1571.[61] Astorre resided in Padua in the late 1550s and was mentioned by a private teacher of music and "letters" as one of his pupils.[62]

The dedication to Venetian citizens also provide some information on informal music making. In dedicating his *Primo libro ... intitulato ll desiderio* to Michele Tron, Bonagiunta says: "It was my good fortune that the other night I came to your Lordship's house, to entertain myself and be restored with some honorable musicians, which was as pleasing as can be to me [...] for the honorable discussions that were held among us."[63] In addition, another dedication, that of *D'Hettor Vidue et d'Alessandro Striggio ... Madrigali a V & VI voci* (RISM 1566[23]), lists as dedicatees Giuseppe Grandonio and Camillo Trevisan. The same two names are found together in a tax document from 1566, where the patrician Carlo Contarini stated that he owned a house on the island of Murano, in the parish of San Salvador, rented to "messer Camillo Trivisan, and messer Iseppo Grandonio, and friends." Houses on Murano were often the retreats of members of the nobility and of the merchant families, and Muranese gardens ("orti") were the place for entertainment of every type. It is possibly in this very house that the Venetian poet Celio Magno presented his compositions.[64] The dedication of Bonagiunta's *Canzone napolitane a tre voci. Secondo libro* (RISM 1566[7]), is also dedicated to a group of Venetian patrons, Marco Milano, Davit Grandonio and Alvise

Grimani, and this joint dedication might also be an indication that the singer had taken part in musical soirées organized by the dedicatees.

A few of Bonagiunta's dedications underline his ties to the Marche: two are to Giovanni Ferro da Macerata and one to Vincenzo Lucchini, bishop of Ancona. While the dedication to Lucchini is an isolated case, those to Giovanni Ferro are much more interesting. The dedication to Ferro of the print in memory of Annibal Caro is understandable in view of the fact that Caro and Ferro were both *marchigiani*, and "cavalieri Loretani," but the dedication to him of a print as important as *Il cicalamento delle donne al bucato*, suggests that Bonagiunta had ties to Ferro, possibly dating from the early part of his career. Ferro's music patronage is confirmed by the fact that he was also the dedicatee of other prints, namely Francesco Adriani's *Primo libro de madrigali a sei voci*, Giovanni Ferretti's *Secondo libro di canzoni napolitane*, and Baldassare Donato's *Secondo libro de madrigali a quattro voci*.[65]

The choices made by Bonagiunta in compiling his anthologies shed some light on the procedures that guided sixteenth-century editors. I have already discussed Bonagiunta's links to some of the most prestigious composers represented in his prints. His habit seems to be to turn always to composers who were readily available, especially (but not exclusively) when selecting the music of the lesser known contributors, so that we see a numerical preponderance of composers active in Venice or in the Marche. One could divide the various composers in several groups.[66] The first consists of the established composers of international fame, for instance Rore, Lasso, de Monte. The second group is a step below, but it consists of composers active and recognized by contemporary purchasers of music books: among these I might put musicians such as Merulo and Porta, or Zarlino (already known as a theorist, but not a prolific composer). The third group includes composers that at the time of the publication would have been known locally, but whose inclusion might not have been helpful (commercially speaking) beyond a limited geographical area. In this group one could put Vincenzo Bell'haver or Daniele Grisonio. The last group is made up of composers so obscure that one has to presume their inclusion depends more on their relationship with the editor, the printer, or the person responsible for financing the print than on their musical merits. Bonagiunta selects a fair number of these, for instance Hettor Vidue and Adriano Anville. In at least one case it is possible to see Bonagiunta's favoritism at work: his 1565 madrigal collection *Le vive fiamme* is made up almost exclusively of pieces by Rore, the lone exception being a piece by Adriano Anville. When this collection went through several reprints, beginning in 1569, every subsequent reprint dropped both the Anville piece and the mention of Bonagiunta's role, adding instead such Rore "hits" as "Da le belle contrade." This suggests that the inclusion of Anville had been determined solely by his friendship with Bonagiunta, rather than by artistic merits. The inclusion of personal friends and favorites is hardly surprising; in fact it seems to be a constant feature of anthologies, both literary and musical, where the appearance of one's work next to those of the great authors allowed to share their immortality.[67]

Vidue's name is prominently displayed in the madrigal collection *D'hettor Vidue et d'Alessandro Striggio ... Madrigali a V & VI voci*, published by Rampazetto in 1566. The prominence of Vidue's name is certainly due to Bonagiunta's friendship with the composer: in the dedication of Lasso's fifth book of motets Bonagiunta links Vidue with Ancona and discusses a visit there when he had spent time with Vidue, whom he calls "conductor [chori moderator] of [the bishop's] choir."[68] It is interesting that the appearance of Vidue's name on the madrigal print predates slightly the dedication of Lasso's motet book to the bishop of Ancona, as if Bonagiunta had tried to ingratiate himself with the bishop in order to gain financial support for the more important Lasso print.

The Vidue-Striggio print is remarkable also for the name of its printer, since Bonagiunta worked primarily with Scotto. Furthermore, the printer's name is missing from the title page of this print, appearing only at the bottom of the *tavola* at the end of each part book. We also know that Rampazetto used to print for other publishers, and I suggest this print's real publisher might have been Scotto, or Bonagiunta himself. The absolute consistency with which all of Bonagiunta's prints are described as "posti in luce" by him, even when he does not claim to have manipulated or corrected the musical text, makes me think that he might have been, at least in part, financially responsible for some of his publications, rather than a simple in-house editor for Scotto or others. This hypothesis is supported by a small item in the records of the church of St. Mark's. On 25 September 1565 Bonagiunta obtained a loan from the Procuratori of the church in the amount of forty ducats.[69] While not extravagant, this sum was a substantial one, equivalent to roughly half his annual salary; in addition the guarantor required by the Procuratori to give a loan to an employee was, in this case, Zuane Griffo (or Griffio), a bookseller and printer.[70] By comparison, the loan received by Merulo before starting his printing business was one hundred ducats.[71] It is possible that forty ducats might have been enough to invest in the printing of one or more music books, especially considering that Bonagiunta (as opposed to Merulo), did not bear the expense of the printing equipment. The lone surviving Venetian music printing contract from the 1560s shows that the sum of eighty-eight ducats and five *lire* would cover all expenses, and presumably the printer's profit for five hundred copies of a music book.[72] Given the possibility of forming a partnership, forty ducats would have enabled Bonagiunta to gain a sizable share of the enterprise. It is worth noting that the first anthology edited by Bonagiunta bears a dedication dated 24 November 1565, almost exactly two months after the date of the loan. The exact nature of the collaboration between the musician and the printer, or printers, is hard to define. Jane Bernstein has already pointed out that several of the Bonagiunta prints, although bearing the name of Girolamo Scotto as printer, bear printer's marks of others, suggesting a wider network of partners.[73] We can say for sure that Bonagiunta chose, edited, and proofread the music, and that, given the documentary evidence, he most likely contributed to the investment. Whether he was also expected to provide the music or not is harder to establish. There is little question in my mind that his references to having been given music by several masters would mean that the enterprising young man had his own stock of music to publish, which might have been one of his greatest assets, far more important than the forty ducats borrowed from the church of St. Mark's. We will also see that it is entirely possible that Bonagiunta, using his own contacts in the music world, might have commissioned some of the music he edited; however, some of his more generic anthologies might have included music that had arrived, one way or another, into Scotto's hands, as I have suggested earlier in the case of works by Stefano Rossetto.

The print which represents Bonagiunta's crowning achievement as editor of music is the madrigal collection *Corona della morte dell'illustre signore ... Annibal Caro*, whose dedication to the *marchigiano* Giovanni Ferro is dated May 25, 1568. The occasion for which all the sonnets in this anthology were written was the death, on November 20, 1566 in Rome, of the Italian writer and humanist Annibal Caro, who was a fellow countryman of Bonagiunta, having been born in 1507 in Civitanova Marche. The wording of the dedication of this collection illustrates Bonagiunta's role:

> " ... I have collected several sonnets composed on the occasion of the death of the excellent Sig. Annibal Caro by Sig. Giovan Battista, his most loving nephew, and, having had them dressed by some excellent composers with music that has harmonies very suitable to the subject of the poems, I want them to go out in the world with the other musical works that have already appeared through my labor: so that they will bear witness to my desire to satisfy ... the friendship I have with his nephew."[74]

Although the *Corona* is not the first "raccolta celebrativa" in music, it is, nevertheless, only the second commemorative anthology in the history of music publishing and the first to be printed in Italy and to memorialize a non-musician.[75] The sonnets of the *Corona* were commissioned from various literary figures: Giovan Battista Zucarino, better known to musicologists for being the author of the texts of the 1586 collection *Corona di dodici sonetti ... alla Gran Duchessa di Toscana*,[76] D. Veniero, surely the Venetian patrician Domenico Venier, who was a patron of the arts and a poet,[77] Girolamo Fenaruolo, whose poems offer an intimate picture of Venetian musical life,[78] and Cardinal Bobba, created cardinal of Aosta in 1565.[79] With the possible exception of Cardinal Bobba, Bonagiunta must have had close ties, or easy access, to all these poets, and it is possible that precisely this familiarity with literary figures gave him the impetus for the production of *Corona della morte*, following a pattern that was already established for anthologies of poetry.[80] Whether the initial idea came from Giovan Battista Caro or from Bonagiunta, the musician was an obvious choice as editor of this collection because of his experience in the music publishing world, his ties to the Marche, and his personal friendship with Giovan Battista.

There is little doubt that this print represents a true "edizione collettiva," in which pre-compositional, non-musical considerations determined to a large extent the shape of the musical anthology. The choice of composers for this anthology is interesting, particularly because Bonagiunta clearly states that he had a role in selecting them. In fact, it is possible that Bonagiunta influenced in some way the compositional process, by suggesting certain solutions to the composers contributing to the anthology.[81] For the most part, Bonagiunta turned to those musicians who were within easy reach. Of the fourteen composers represented, five were in Venice at the time (Zarlino, Grisonio, A. Gabrieli, Bell'haver, Merulo), four certainly (or most likely) in the Venetian territories (Comis in or around Treviso, Raimondo in Vicenza, Sperindio and Renaldi in Padua), and three were originally from the Marche (or working there in 1568) and could have been acquainted not only with both Caro and Bonagiunta, but also with the patron of this print, Giovanni Ferro (Schietti, Ghibellini, Adriani). The two exceptions are Palestrina, who nevertheless must have had occasion to meet Caro or his nephew in Rome, and Anville (possibly the same musician as Adriano Hawill or d'Hawille) who, as I have shown earlier, had already managed to have some of his pieces entered in collections edited by Bonagiunta.

The physical appearance of this print shows a great deal of care on the part of the printer. The collection is printed in the upright quarto format of the other Scotto anthologies of the late 1560s. The title page bears an unusual device, with two *putti* holding a scroll with the motto "Virtus in omni re dominatur," and an inscription within the central frame that reads: "Ioannes Ferrus miles Sancti Georgii." It is obvious that this is a special device, designed to highlight the dedicatee's role in the production of the print: no other Bonagiunta collection I have seen bears a device not traceable to a printer or publisher. It would have been very appropriate for Ferro to underwrite a large portion of the cost of a print that was to honor one of his countrymen and colleagues. As further evidence of the care lavished in the printing of this anthology, in the canto part book (but not in the others) each madrigal is preceded by a page on which the text of the poem is printed, framed by decorative wood block motifs.

One of the most interesting questions regarding Bonagiunta's activities as an editor is how he became such a central figure in Venetian music publishing in the 1560s. Surely there was no shortage of competent musicians in Venice, and in fact the musicians of the city had sporadically engaged in publishing projects. Moreover, Bonagiunta was not particularly comfortable financially, and thus able to finance editions out of his own pocket, the way other singers of St. Mark's could have. Perhaps it was easier for an outsider, a recent immigrant to Venice, to grasp the potential of the print medium and to wish to explore more fully some of its possibilities. Other factors that must have contributed to his success are his extensive travels and personal contacts with a wide circle of musicians (which might have resulted in a well stocked personal library), his friendship and association with many respected literary figures, and his willingness to make a personal financial investment in the business. It is possible that Bonagiunta had an influence on Merulo's decision to begin a publishing career: certainly the example of a musician combining successfully service at St. Mark's and the demands of the Venetian publishing world must have been on Merulo's mind. More importantly, it is to the foresight of Scotto and Bonagiunta that we owe the establishment of a truly modern framework for the dissemination of music through the establishment of a new type of musical anthology. It is in the 1560s that the Venetian press really embraces a new attitude towards the production of anthologies, which treats these collections as much more than technically advanced versions of manuscripts. The use of self-conscious marketing strategies, the increased role of the professional editor (and the increased public recognition of his or her role),[82] the greater involvement of the composer in the planning stages of a collection, the development of prospective and retrospective anthologies, are all symptoms of this changed attitude, which led the Venetian press towards the industrialization of the late sixteenth century.

Endnotes

* Research for this article was supported by grants from the Gladys Krieble Delmas Foundation. I wish to thank Dr. Elizabeth Teviotdale and Prof. Jane Bernstein (who also generously shared some of her research with me) for several helpful suggestions on an earlier draft, and Prof. Margaret Rosenthal for a crucial bibliographic reference.

1   "Il Cinquecento e il Seicento," in *Letteratura italiana*, ed. Alberto Asor Rosa (Torino: Einaudi, 1982-1990), 6:342, n. 21. A few recent studies have examined sixteenth-century musical anthologies. The most pertinent to the present article is included in Franco Piperno's *Gli 'Eccellentissimi musici della città di Bologna', con uno studio sull'antologia madrigalistica del Cinquecento* (Firenze: Olschki, 1985); see especially pp. 1–42. See also the brief contribution of Marco Giuliani, "Antologie, miscellanee, edizioni collettive nei secc. XVI-XVII," *Nuova Rivista Musicale Italiana* 22/1 (1988): 70–76, which attempts to refine further Piperno's terminology.

2   RISM 1569[20]. It includes, among others, pieces by Rore, Willaert, Donato, de Vento, della Viola, Berchem, and Perissone Cambio. Throughout this article in referring to sixteenth-century music prints I will use the sigla given in *Répertoire International des Sources Musicales*, B/I, *Recueils imprimés XVIe-XVIIe siècles*, ed. F. Lesure (München: Henle, 1960), and A/I, *Einzeldrucke vor 1800*, ed. O. Albrecht and K.H. Schlager (Kassel: Bärenreiter, 1971–1986).

3   James Haar, *Essays on Italian Poetry and Music in the Renaissance. 1350–1600*, (Berkeley: University of California Press, 1986), 130. As an example of the deliberate "retrospective" character of some earlier French collections one could cite RISM 1536[2] and 1536[3]: *Premier livre contenant XXXI chansons musicales esleues de plusieurs livres par cy-devant imprimez* and *Second livre contenant XXXI chansons musicales esleues de plusieurs livres par cy-devant imprimez*, both printed by Attaingnant in Paris. The wording of these title pages is unusual, considering that almost all other collections of French chansons of the period make a point to advertise the inclusion of "chansons nouvelles" on their title page. A couple of slightly later French collections go even further in advertising the age of their contents. In 1560 Le Roy and Ballard printed the *Livre des Meslanges, contenant six vingtz chansons ... soit des autheurs antiques, soit des plus memorables de nostre temps* (See François Lesure and Geneviève Thibault, *Bibliographie des éditions d'Adrian Le Roy et Robert Ballard (1551–1598)* (Paris: Société Française de Musicologie, 1955), 91–4). The same publishers printed in 1572 the *Mellange de chansons tant des vieux autheurs que des modernes* (RISM 1572[2]).

4   A few examples among many possible: RISM 1563[16], *Di Pietro Vinci ... il primo libro di madrigali a cinque voci* (Venezia: Scotto), which includes 14 madrigals by Vinci and one by Giulio Severino; RISM 1565[16], *Il primo et secondo libro de madrigali a cinque, et a sei voci, di Giovan Leonardo Primavera* (Venezia: Scotto), which contains 16 madrigals by Primavera and one by Striggio. While bibliographically justifiable the arrangement of the RISM volume *Recueils imprimés, XVIe-XVII siècles* is an obstacle to the establishment of a taxonomy of the sixteenth-century music anthology, because it obscures the issue by including collections which are anthologies only according to the bibliographic guidelines of its compilers.

5   On the lyric poetry anthologies, see Louis George Clubb and William G. Clubb, "Building a Lyric Canon: Gabriel Giolito and the Rival Anthologists, 1545–1590," *Italica* 68

(1991): 332–44. Note 1 of that article contains a summary of literature on the subject of Italian lyric poetry anthologies.

6   See Amedeo Quondam, *Il naso di Laura* (Ferrara: IRS, Franco Cosimo Panini, 1991), 108 ff.

7   The prominent role of the Venetian press in the production of musical anthologies is mirrored in its output of poetic anthologies. According to statistics presented by Amedeo Quondam (*Il naso di Laura*, 115), virtually all collections of poetry published in Italy in the years between 1531 and 1550 were produced in Venice. For the period 1551-70 the percentage falls somewhat, but remains at over two thirds of all such collections published in Italy.

8   The earliest printed poetic "edizione collettiva," or rather, "raccolta celebrativa," was the 1504 collection of poetry for the death of Serafino Aquilano, *Collectanee grece, latine et vulgari per diversi autori moderni nella morte dell'ardente Serafino Aquilano* (Bologna: Bazalieri), edited by Giovanni Filoteo Achillini, which predates by several decades similar musical anthologies (See A. Quondam, *Il naso di Laura*, 136). I think that the first musical collection to show a similar frame of mind is RISM 1539[25], *Musiche fatte nelle nozze dello illustrissimo Duca di Firenze il signor Cosimo de Medici et della illustrissima consorte sua mad. Leonora da Tolleto* (Venezia: A. Gardano), in which music that formerly might have been confined to a court manuscript is duplicated and offered to the public, as a testimony, not only to contemporaries, but also to posterity, of the magnificence of the Medicis.

9   The most famous and largest of these collections is *Tempio alla divina signora donna Giovanna d'Aragona* (Venezia: Pietrasanta, 1555), edited by Girolamo Ruscelli, which stretches to 626 pages and includes 473 poems. I am aware that a parallel in music can also be made with presentation manuscripts, but I think that the differences between these manuscripts and the celebratory printed collections are greater than the similarities, and that the ties between poetic and musical prints of this type are in fact very strong.

10 On occasion, it seems that the editor or publisher derived the title of a musical anthology from a poetic line found in one of the pieces, but it is interesting that when subsequent volumes by the same title exist, they do not show a similar link between title and contents, suggesting that only marketing considerations were guiding the choice of the title. For instance RISM 1566[2], *Primo libro de diversi eccellent.mi autori a quattro voci. Intitulato Il desiderio* (Venice: Scotto), opens with Rore's madrigal "Il desiderio e la speranza," which was probably the inspiration for the title. The two later madrigal anthologies that use this title (RISM 1566[3] and 1567[16]) do not include any pieces that might justify it.

11 RISM 1517[2], (Roma: A. Antico & N. Giudici).

12 Respectively RISM 1582[5] (Ferrara: V. Baldini), 1570[15] (Venezia: G. Scotto), 1566[2] (Venezia: G. Scotto, 1586[12] (Venezia: herede di G. Scotto), 1565[18] (Venezia: G. Scotto).

13 RISM 1569[19] (Venezia: G. Scotto).

14 These are the various *Libri delle Muse* (RISM 1555[25], 1557[17], 1558[12], 1559[16], 1559[17], 1559[18]) and three books of *Motetti del Laberinto* (RISM 1554[14], 1554[15], 1555[16]). See Appendix 1 for a complete list of anthologies meeting these criteria.

15   There are, of course, several pseudo-anthologies listed in RISM that do not follow this practice, but for reasons I have already explained, these ought to be regarded as single composer prints, rather than actual anthologies.

16   Haar, *Essays in Italian Poetry*, 130–1.

17   It is interesting that the almost total preponderance of printed versus manuscript anthologies in sixteenth-century music is not matched by a similar trend in poetic anthologies. Even with the development of printed anthologies of poetry, manuscript collections continued to be assembled and circulated, more extensively (as far as we can tell) than musical manuscript anthologies. Obviously I am not referring to the dissemination of music in manuscript, which continued, but to the preparation by an editor of a bona fide manuscript anthology. On some of these problems see Amedeo Quondam, *Il naso di Laura*, 135–6.

18   For a discussion of the establishment of the printers' guild, see Horatio F. Brown, *The Venetian Printing Press* (London: J.C. Nimmo, 1891), 83. One interesting point about the guild, made to me by Prof. Jane Bernstein in a personal communication, is that its first board (presided by Girolamo Scotto), was dominated by printers with strong business associations with the Scotto firm.

19   See Jane Bernstein, "Financial Arrangements and the Role of Printer and Composer in Sixteenth-Century Italian Music Printing," *Acta Musicologica*, 63 (1991): 43.

20   The speculation about Giolito is found in L. George Clubb and W.G. Clubb, "Building a Lyric Canon," 332–3. In many archival documents I have seen, Scotto is often called "mercator," rather than "bibliopola" or "impressor" as were those who were active only in the book trade. See for instance the documents in Archivio di Stato di Venezia (henceforth I-Vas), Notarile Atti, Busta 11874, Notaio B. Solianis (1564–65). Many of these documents have no direct connection with the book trade. Incidentally, the increased number of anthologies was not the only change for Scotto's business: from 1564 his music was consistently printed in the upright format he first used in 1544 for a few prints, for instance Anton Francesco Doni's *Dialogo della musica* (RISM 1544[22]), but one he never employed again until 1564. Both these changes might be seen as evidence of Scotto's business instinct: the production of anthologies because it represents a conscious effort to market music in a "modern" way, and the new format probably because, according to the hypothesis of Prof. Bernstein, it might have resulted in some cost savings. It is interesting that while virtually all other changes in print production introduced by either Gardano or Scotto were immediately copied by the other, the consistent use of this new format is one change that other Venetian printers, including Gardano, did not imitate until the 1570s.

21   Willaert's print is *Intavolatura de li madrigali di Verdelotto da cantare et sonare nel lauto, intavolati per Messer Adriano* (Venezia: Ottaviano Scotto, 1536; RISM V 1224). Another interesting case is that of the singer Francesco di Conforti, employed by the ducal chapel, who petitioned the Venetian Collegio in 1504 and 1510 for printing privileges for the publication of non-musical books. The list of projected publications and some allusions to semi-official governmental printing contracts indicate that Francesco was a serious practitioner of the trade. See I-Vas, Collegio, Notatorio, Reg. 15, fol. 109r-v, and Reg. 16, fol. 70r.

22   See the remarks by Rebecca Edwards in her "Claudio Merulo: Servant of the State and Musical Entrepreneur in Later Sixteenth-Century Venice" (Ph.D. diss., Princeton University, 1990), 162. I think one can also see in the 1560s more frequent examples of

musicians acting as editors for prints of music by a single composer. One of the examples more pertinent to this discussion is a collection of motets by Zarlino, *Modulationes sex vocum* (Venezia: Rampazetto, 1566; RISM Z 100), whose contents are said to be "per Philippum Iusbertum ... colectae, ac per eundem nunc primum in publicum datae." For information on Filippo Iusberti (or Zusberti), who was a singer at St. Mark's under Zarlino, see my dissertation, "The Chapel of St. Mark's at the Time of Adrian Willaert (1527–1562): A Documentary Study," (Ph.D. diss., University of North Carolina at Chapel Hill, 1986), 362–3 and 365–6. It is unclear why Zarlino did not choose to publish his own works, but it is likely, in my opinion, that he felt a direct involvement with a project of this type to be somewhat beneath the dignity of his newly acquired status as *maestro*.

23 *Di Baldesar Donato il secondo libro de madrigali a quattro voci* (Venezia: Scotto, 1568; RISM D 3415): "ho conferito con M. Giulio Bonagiunta, cantor di S. Marco, questo mio disegno." Donato probably mentioned Bonagiunta in this dedication because he dedicated his print to Giovanni Ferro da Macerata, who was (as we shall see later) a patron of Bonagiunta. In the preface Donato also states that he had been putting away for future use those four-voice madrigals of his that were judged (by himself and by other connoisseurs) as being "più artificiosi delli altri."

24 On the literary editors, see the important contribution of Claudia Di Filippo Bareggi, *Il mestiere di scrivere. Lavoro intellettuale e mercato librario a Venezia nel Cinquecento* (Roma: Bulzoni, 1988).

25 The main secondary sources on Bonagiunta are entries in standard reference works: Denis Arnold, *Die Musik in Geschichte und Gegenwart*, Supplement, s.v. "Bonagiunta, Giulio;" and *The New Grove Dictionary of Music and Musicians*, s.v. "Bonagiunta, Giulio;" Liliana Pannella, *Dizionario Biografico degli Italiani* (Roma: Istituto della Enciclopedia Italiana, 1960-), s.v. "Bonagiunta, Giulio." The last is by far the most extensive article on Bonagiunta.

26 Pannella, "Bonagiunta, Giulio," does mention that the composer's ties to literary and musical figures from the Marche might lead one to believe him a Marchigiano, but she considers this hypothesis less likely.

27 "[...] mi pareria di meritare non poco biasimo, se con la mia industria non procurassi di ampliare, & publicare, in quanto io posso, le lodi delli miei compatrioti, come essi con le sue virtuose fatiche hanno illustrato, & honorato la sua & mia patria."

28 On Caro, see C. Mutini *Dizionario Biografico degli Italiani*, s.v. "Caro, Annibal."

29 *Quintus liber concentuum sacrorum ... quinis, senis, octonis vocibus decantandis* (Venezia: C. Correggiatem, 1568, RISM L 818): "Quatuor abhinc annos cum in patriam rediens Ancona transirem ibique triduum comoratus essem, Hector vidue musicus ac tui chori moderator me ad osculandam tibi manum duxit." I think that the position of Vidue was the equivalent of the *maestro di coro*, namely the individual responsible for the smooth functioning of all liturgy, otherwise Bonagiunta would have said "Magister capellae." There are examples at St. Mark's in Venice of musically inclined *maestri di coro*.

30 This information is available in Floriano Grimaldi's *La cappella musicale di Loreto nel Cinquecento*, (Loreto: Ente Rassegne Musicali, 1981), 36–7. There is at least one more document in Grimaldi's book (pp. 88-9) that surely refers to Bonagiunta, although it is not identified as such. A letter of April 1, 1563, from the Venetian organ maker Alessandro Vesentin dal Palazzo to the Governor of the Santa Casa explains the reasons for the delay in sending an "organetto," among others the need to find a suitable person

to accompany it on its journey, a person now found in the person of "messer Giulio chantor qui in Santo Marco." Giulio Bonagiunta is the only Giulio among the singers of St. Mark's for the period in question. Other documents in the archives of St. Mark's and the dedication of RISM L 818 (see previous footnote) probably refer to this trip.

31   I-Vas, Procuratori di San Marco de Supra, ACTORUM, Reg. 129, fol. 136v.

32   Pannella, "Bonagiunta, Giulio."

33   I-Vas, Procuratori di San Marco de Supra, Giornali Cassier, Reg. 3, 10 April 1568: "counted to *ser* Iulio Bonagiunta, singer, five ducats, given for his trip to Bavaria by order of the Most Illustrious Cashier." [contadi a ser Iulio bonagiunta cantor ducati cinque dete per il suo viazo di Baviera de ordine del Clarisimo Cassier].

34   For instance, a 1565 document, dated 21 April (I-Vas, Procuratori di San Marco de Supra, Actorum, Reg. 130, fol. 79r), tells us that Bonagiunta and another contralto, Gherardo Molino, had left the chapel, but a later document (23 May; *ibid.*, fol. 83v) contradicts the earlier one, implying that their absence had been a temporary one. The last dedication signed by Bonagiunta in Venice is dated June 5, 1568; the dedication of RISM L 818, also printed in 1568, does not bear a date.

35   Hellmut Federhofer, *Musikpflege und Musiker am Grazer Habsburgerhof der Erzherzöger Karl und Ferdinand von Innerösterreich (1564–1619)*, (Mainz, B. Schotts Söhne, 1967), 72. Bonagiunta also received a payment of 100 crowns from the agent of the Archduke on 24 February 1568, possibly for music prints, *Ibid.*, 231.

36   I-Vas, Collegio, Notatorio, Reg. 37, fol. 38r, dated 1 February 1567 (m.v., i.e. 1568). In this document the Procuratori reaffirm a salary increase for Bonagiunta of twenty ducats a year, making him, at one hundred ducats a year, one of the highest paid singers. The Procuratori also state that the increase was to have begun on the date of his rehiring (not specified, but between 17 December 1566 and 14 May 1567; no document of this sort has survived), fixing, very generously, such date "when he left Bavaria through the letters of our Procuratori of the Church of St. Mark's." Bonagiunta was then given the equivalent of two months of salary to cover the period between his departure from Bavaria and the date of his official rehiring. Even more surprising, given the Procuratori's oft-stated position in similar cases, this proposal passed unanimously.

37   I-Vas, Santo Stefano, Busta 4, fol. 33v, and fol. 35r.

38   I-Vas, Esecutori alla Bestemmia, Notatorio Terminazioni, Busta 56, fol. 31r, 28 May 1567. The other person involved was a "pre Luca francigena:" at the time there was a French singer and priest at St. Mark's by the name of Luca Galterio, who was often called simply "Luca francigena."

39   See R. Pelicelli, "Musicisti in Parma nei secoli XV-XVI," *Note d'archivio per la storia musicale* 9 (1932): 118–9.

40   The print is *Orlandi Lassi, Adriani Hawill, ac nonnullorum aliorum musicorum Missae* (Milano: Francesco & eredi di Simone Tini; RISM 1588[4]).

41   *Quinque missae suavissimis modulationibus refertae ... authore Orlando Lasso* (Venezia: C. da Correggio, 1570; RISM L 831). The 1588 Milanese reprint (Rism L 984) has an identical title page.

42   Other examples of what one could call "local" Milanese additions to works of other composers are, for instance: *Missarum 5 vocum ... auctore Orpheo Vecchio ... quibus accessit Missa Jac. Antonii Piccioli, Liber primus* (Milano: Francesco et heredes di S. Tini; RISM 1588[1]); and *Li soavissimi Responsorii della Settimana Santa a 5 voci*, by

Vincenzo Ruffo, but containing a small number of compositions by the much less known Agostino Resta (Milano: Francesco & heredi di S. Tini; RISM 1586[5]).

43   As examples of this type of print from Merulo's press, I can cite *Il primo libro de madrigali ... a cinque voci* of Guglielmo Textoris (Venezia: C. da Coreggio et Fausto Bethanio, 1566; RISM T 600); the *Madrigali di Giulio Fiesco ... a cinque voci. Libro secondo* (Venezia: C. da Coreggio, 1967; RISM F 716); the *Madrigali di Giovan Battista Conforti ... a cinque voci. Libro primo* (Venezia: C. da Coreggio, 1967; RISM C 3497); and *Madrigali di Domenico Micheli da Bologna ... a sei voci. Libro terzo* (Venezia: C. da Coreggio, 1567; RISM M 2678). It seems to me that in every such case a struggling printer would not have undertaken the task of publishing the collection without some assurance as to the financial arrangements, for Merulo could not have expected a return comparable to that of his Lasso, Arcadelt and Verdelot prints.

44   Some Scotto anthologies published between 1562 and 1565 are so similar in character to some of Bonagiunta's collections that it is tempting to speculate (although there is no documentary evidence to support this) that Bonagiunta might have served as uncredited in-house editor for the firm prior to 1565.

45   *Quintus liber concentuum sacrorum ... quinis, senis, octonis vocibus decantandis* (Venezia: apud Claudium Correggiatem, 1568; RISM L 818): "cum ab Orlando Lasso ... multis musicis compositionis ea lege donatus fuerim, ut ad meum arbitrium eas ipsas imprimendas curarem."

46   "Orlando è qui, et sta bene, allegro et bon compagnon a tutti, partirà fra 8 giorni di qui per Ferrara con una muta di madrigali, che l'ha fatto stampare e dedicato a quel duca. Vedremo come sarà liberale." This is confirmed in a letter from Ferrara by Lorenzo Canigiani to the Duke of Florence, dated 9 June 1567, which tells us: "We had here Orlando di Lasso ... and he has given to the Duke certain printed madrigals of his, receiving little reward and satisfaction from that Most Illustrious Signore." [Ecci stato Orlando di Lassus ... et ha indiritto et donato certi suoi madrigali in stampa al Sr. Duca con portarne poca mancia et sodisfactione di quello Ill.mo Signore], These letters are quoted in Horst Leuchtmann, *Orlando di Lasso: Sein Leben* (Wiesbaden: Breitkopf & Härtel, 1976, 138–9; and also in Wolfgang Boetticher, *Orlando di Lasso und seine Zeit* (Kassel: Bärenreiter, 1958), 164. The identification of the print is already included in Bernstein, "Financial arrangements," 54–5.

47   The question of how various printers and editors managed to acquire music by famous composers is, of course, a very interesting one. As far as Lasso is concerned, there are other instances of editors acquiring sizable quantities of his music, though not necessarily directly from the composer. See, for instance RISM 1557[22], *Secondo libro delle Muse, a cinque voci, Madrig. d'Orlando di Lassus* (Roma: A. Barré), edited by Giovanbattista Bruno, who states in the dedication: "Finding myself many days ago in Spoleto, I happened to acquire many madrigals by Orlando di Lasso, ... and having kept them with me for a long time I was moved by the entreaties of several *virtuosi* not to hide them any longer." [Ritrovandomi molti giorni o sono in Spoleti, mi vennero per aventura a le mani molti Madrigalli d'Orlando Lassus, ... quali havendoli tenuto appresso me longo tempo me disposi a preghi d'infiniti virtuosi di non tenerli più occulti].

48   See earlier, p. 52–53 for a discussion of evidence of Bonagiunta's trips abroad in this period.

49   "cum ab Orlando Lasso ... cantiones aliquae, vulgo Mottetta nuncupata mihi donata

fuissent, quibus authoris liberalitate mihi pro meis uti licet, typis mandare ... publicareque volui."

50   "per la gran familiarità, & amorevol servitù, che io longo tempo ho tenuta con l'eccellentiss. Musico M. Cipriano Rore, benignamente per sua cortesia mi fece partecipe d'alcuni suoi bellissimi Madrigali, a quattro, & a cinque voci, pregandomi li dovesse tenir appresso di me, accio le sue opere non così facilmente nelle mani di ciascheduno si divulgassero." Bonagiunta justified what seems to be a breach of the composer's trust by stating that after Rore's death he wanted the world to see these compositions.

51   A very good example of a print where the music was probably commissioned directly by the editor will be discussed later in this article.

52   *Il lamento d'Olimpia ... con una canzone del medesimo, a quattro, a cinque, a sei, a sette, a otto, a nove, & dieci voci*, RISM R 2729.

53   de Monte assumed his position at the Viennese court on May 1, 1568 (see Milton Steinhardt and Robert M. Lindell, *The New Grove Dictionary*, s.v. "Monte, Philippe de," 505). The route between Rome and Vienna could not fail to pass at least through Venetian territories, if not through Venice.

54   The dedicatees are listed with their respective collections in Appendix 2.

55   RISM G 60: *Di Andrea Gabrieli ... il primo libro di madrigali a cinque voci* (Venezia: Figliuoli di Antonio Gardano, 1572). Despite the presence of a dedication, this is a reprint of a 1566 Gardano edition (RISM G 59).

56   Villabruna is also the dedicatee of Giovanni Zappasorgo's *Napolitane a 3 voci, libro primo* (Venezia: Scotto, 1571; RISM Z 93).

57   "... in this period, having sowed some of my musical seeds in the fertile ground of the Magnificent Roncale family, thanks to the help of Messer Giovanni Molino, and seeing the fruit born, because of the care and esteem that they had and have for it ..." [trovandomi a questi giorni haver seminato alcune mie semenze Musicale in Rovigo nel fertile terreno della Magnifica Casa Roncale, mercè da l'aiuto de Meser Giovanni Molino, & vedendo il frutto, che n'è nasciuto per il conto & stima, che n'hanno fatto & fanno] *Il gaudio, primo libro de madrigali de diversi ... a tre voci* (Vinegia: Appresso Girolamo Scotto, 1567). The flowery language of the dedication makes it fairly ambiguous. It is possible that Bonagiunta is referring to an actual visit to Rovigo, or that his "musical seeds" are the pieces of his *Terzo libro del desiderio* (RISM 1567[16]) dedicated to Antonio Roncale: the dedication of this collection is dated 11 June 1567, that of *Il gaudio* 1 October 1567. The announcement of the discovery of this previously unknown edition of *Il gaudio* in the Torrefranca collection of the Conservatorio Benedetto Marcello in Venice (I-Vc) appeared in Bernstein, "Financial Arrangements," 53. I wish to thank Prof. Bernstein for putting her transcriptions of the title page and dedication at my disposal. The 1567 edition is not listed in any currently available bibliography, but will be listed in Prof. Bernstein's study of the Scotto printing firm. The later, known, edition of *Il gaudio* (Venezia: herede di G. Scotto, 1586; RISM 1586[12]) does not bear any mention of Bonagiunta's role.

58   A letter from a Venetian envoy, written shortly after Dorimbergo's Imperial appointment to oversee the Friuli region, described him in the following terms: "The other envoy, Signor Vido di Dorimberg, is noble, and a native of Gorizia, and all his lands are in that area; he is thought to be a person of good intelligence, very skillful, tractable,

and very compassionate." I-Vas, Ambasciatori, Dispacci Germania, Filza +, no. 54, letter of Giovanni Micheli from Prague on July 4, 1562: "L'altro commissario, il Signor Vido di Dorimberg, è nobile, et nativo di Gorizia, et ha tutto'l suo là, tenuto persona di buono ingegno, molto destra, et trattabile, et di molta humanità."

59 *Il primo libro de madrigali a quarto voci* (Gardano, 1570; RISM B 735) Ludovico Balbi, a singer sometimes confused with his nephew Alvise, was at St. Mark's between 1568 and 1570.

60 See Walter Senn, *Musik und Theater am Hof zu Innsbruck* (Innsbruck: Oesterreichische Verlagsanstalt, 1954), 116. Regarding this episode we must also keep in mind that the Friulian Dorimbergo must have kept a close watch on the affairs of San Giovanni dei Furlani [i.e. Friulani], and was therefore eminently qualified to report on Vincenzo, not only from the musical standpoint.

61 For information on Astorre see Astur Baleonus [i.e. Astorre Baglioni], *I Baglioni* (Prato: [Baglioni?], 1964), especially p. 178.

62 See I-Vas, Sant'Uffizio, Busta 15, Proc. 49 ("Francesco Scudieri"). In his deposition to the Inquisitor, Francesco Scudieri mentions him as his student in Latin, but does not say whether he also taught him music. I am presently working on an article which will examine the activities of this music teacher, and the holdings of his library.

63 "Volse la mia buona sorte, ch'io l'altra sera venesse in casa di V. Sig. a pigliar spasso, et consolatione, con alcuni honorati Musici, il che mi fu tanto grato quanto dir si possi ... per li ragionamenti honorati, che fra noi occorsero."

64 The tax declaration, for the so called "Decima," is found in I-Vas, Cinque Savi alle Decime, Busta 134, no. 902. The reference to Celio Magno reading his poetry in Camillo Trevisan's Muranese house is in Pompeo Molmenti, *La storia di Venezia nella vita privata* (Bergamo: Istituto Italiano d'Arti Grafiche, 1925), 2:203.

65 *Il primo libro de madrigali a sei voci di Francesco Adriani* (Venezia: G. Scotto, 1568; RISM A 310); *Di Giovan Ferretti il secondo libro delle canzoni alla napolitana a cinque voci* (Venezia: G. Scotto, 1569; RISM F 518); *Di Baldesar Donato il secondo libro de madrigali a quattro voci* (Venezia: Scotto, 1568; RISM D 3415).

66 For a similar division in lyric poetry anthologies, see L. George Clubb and W.G. Clubb, "Building a Lyric Canon," 336, and A. Quondam, *Il naso di Laura*, 132 and ff., especially 135. On the basis of programmatic prefaces by sixteenth-century editors and using their terminology, Quondam divides the contributors to lyric poetry anthologies in "dotti, intendenti, mezzani, e novelli." Even accounting for the appropriate differences between writing poetry and composing madrigals, this division is valid for musical anthologies.

67 See L. George Clubb and W.G. Clubb, "Building a Lyric Canon," 334.

68 See earlier, note 29.

69 I-Vas, Procuratori di Supra di S. Marco, Reg. 130, fol. 95r.

70 The case for Griffo's ties to music publishing is strengthened by the discovery that he was the arbitrator for Merulo's sale of his publishing business (see Edwards, "Claudio Merulo," 200) and by his strong ties to the Scotto firm. On the association between Scotto and Griffo around 1545–47, see Jane Bernstein, "The Burning Salamander: Assigning a Printer to Some Sixteenth-Century Music Prints," *Notes* 42/3 (March 1986); 491.

71 Edwards, "Claudio Merulo," 159.

72   See Richard Agee, "The Privilege and Venetian Music Printing in the Sixteenth Century" (Ph.D. diss., Princeton University, 1982), 335–6.

73   Bernstein, "Financial Arrangements," 53.

74   "[...] ho raccolto alquanti sonetti composti sopra la morte dell'eccellente Sig. Anibal Caro dal Sig. Giovan Battista suo amantissimo nipote, li quali havendo fatto vestire da eccellenti Compositori d'una Musica, che rende concenti molto proprij alli concetti delle parole, ho voluto che vadano per il mondo con le altre opere Musicali che per mia industria sono state messe in luce: accioche rendano testimonio del mio desiderio di satisfar [...] all'amicitia ch'io tengo col suo nipote." Giovan Battista Caro was the principal heir of his uncle's estate: he was responsible for publishing several works left in manuscript form at his uncle's death.

75   The first printed musical epitaph is, I think, *In epitaphiis Gasparis Othmari* (Nürnberg: Berg & Neuber?; RISM [1554][30]). The idea of such a tribute might have stemmed from Othmayr's own print *Epitaphium D. Martini Lutheri* (Nürnberg: Berg & Neuber, 1546; RISM O 259).

76   (Venezia: Gardano; RISM 1586[11]).

77   On Venier's ties to musical circles, see Martha Feldman, "The Academy of Domenico Venier, Music's Literary Muse in Mid-Cinquecento Venice," *Renaissance Quarterly*, 44/3 (Autumn 1991): 476–512.

78   See his *Rime di Mons. Girolamo Fenaruolo* (Venezia, 1574). He was the dedicatee of Antonino Barges *villotte* (Venezia: Gardano; RISM 1550/18, RISM B 922).

79   Conrad Euber, *Hierarchia Catholica Medii Aevi* (Monasteri, sumptibus et typis librariae Regensbergianae, 1898–1910), 3:46. Bobba died in 1575.

80   Particularly intriguing is Bonagiunta's close friendship with Zucarino, which the editor reveals in the dedication of his *Primo libro degli eterni mottetti* (RISM 1567[3]): "having collected several motets ... I was considering under which shield and protection I should publish them ... when ... discussing this idea of mine, as I often do, with the honored *Messer* Giovan Battista Zucarino, my dear friend ..." [havendo fatto raccolta d'alcuni Mottetti ... tra me stesso stava pensando sotto, che scudo, & protettione, dovessi mandarli in luce ... quando ... ragionando di questo mio pensiero, come soglio far spesso, con l'honorato M. Giovan Battista Zucarino, mio caro amico ...]

81   For instance, there is a remarkable consistency of mode and clef arrangements among the various pieces, far more than what is observable in other Bonagiunta anthologies, suggesting that the editor might have given guidelines to the composers.

82   Lest the reader thinks that I am using "his or her" only to be politically correct, I must point out that Antonio Molino's second book of four-voice madrigals (Venezia: A. Gardano, 1569; RISM M 2948) bears a dedication signed by Maddalena Casulana, who seems to have acted as editor for this print.

APPENDIX 1

Venetian Anthologies with Descriptive Titles, 1550–1570

1554^{14} *Motetti del Laberinto. Libro secondo*, 4vv. (Scotto)

1554^{15} *Motetti del Laberinto. Libro terzo*, 4vv. (Scotto)

1554^{16} *Motetti del Laberinto. Libro quarto*, 5vv. (Scotto)

1555^{15} *Moteti de la fama. Libro primo*, 4vv. (Scotto)

1555^{25} *Il primo libro de le Muse*, 5vv. madrigals (Gardano)

1557^{17} *Madrigali ariosi ... Libro primo delle Muse*, 4vv. (Gardano)

1558^{12} *Madrigali aierosi ... Libro primo delle Muse*, 4vv. (Scotto)

1559^{16} *Il secondo libro de le Muse*, 5vv. (Gardano)

1559^{17} *Secondo libro delle muse, madrigali ariosi*, 4vv. (Scotto)

1559^{18} *Madrigali ariosi. Libro primo delle muse*, 4vv. (Gardano; reprinted (1565^{10}) without the second part of the title)

1559^{19} *Il secondo libro de villotte del fiore alla padoana* (Gardano)

1560^{11} *Il secondo libro de villotte ... intitolate Villotte del fiore* (Scotto)

1561^{8} *Il primo libro de le Muse*, 5vv. (Scotto; = 1555^{25})

1561^{9} *Il secondo libro de le Muse*, 5vv. (Scotto; = 1559^{16})

1561^{10} *Il terzo libro delle Muse*, 5vv. (Gardano)

1562^{2} *Motetti del frutto ... Libro primo*, 4vv. (Scotto)

1562^{5} *I dolci et harmoniosi concenti ... Libro primo*, 5vv. (Scotto)

1562^{6} *I dolci et harmoniosi concenti ... Libro secondo*, 5vv. (Scotto)

1562^{8} *Il primo libro delle muse*, 3vv. (Scotto)

1562^{9} *Il terzo libro delle Muse*, 3vv. (Scotto)

1563^{3} *Liber primus Musarum ... sacrarum cantionum*, 4vv. (Rampazetto)

1563^{7} *Musica spirituale, libro primo* (Scotto)

1563^{9} *Libro terzo delle Muse*, 4vv. (Rampazetto; = 1562^{7}, Roma: Barré)

1564^{14}
1564^{14a} *Il primo libro de villotte ... intitolate Villotte del fiore* (Scotto)

1565^{18} *Le vive fiamme*, 5vv. (Scotto)

1566^{2} *Primo libro ... intitulato Il desiderio*, 4vv. (Scotto)

1566^{3} *Il desiderio. Secondo libro de madrigali*, 5vv. (Scotto)

1566^{4} *Villotte alla padoana .. intitolate Villotte del fiore* (Rampazetto; = 1560^{11})

1567^{13} *Secondo libro delle fiamme*, 5 and 6vv. (Scotto)

1567^{16} *Terzo libro del desiderio*, 4vv. (Scotto)

1567^{23} *Il cicalamento delle donne al bucato* (Scotto)

[1567] *Il Gaudio. primo libro de madrigali*, 3vv. (Scotto)

1568^{2} *Novi thesauri musici, liber primus* (Gardano)

1568^{3} *Novi atque catholici thesauri musici. Liber secundus* (Gardano)

1568[4]   *Novi atque catholici thesauri musici. Liber tertius* (Gardano)

1568[5]   *Novi atque catholici thesauri musici. Liber quartus* (Gardano)

1568[6]   *Liber quintus & ultimus* (Gardano)

1568[12]   *Il terzo libro delle fiamme,* 5vv. (Scotto)

1568[13]   *Gli amorosi concenti, Primo libro,* 4vv. (Scotto)

1568[16]   *Corona della morte dell'illustre signore. il ... commendator Anibal Caro* (Scotto)

1569[2]   *Motectarum divinitatis. Liber primus* (Merulo)

1569[18]   *Il terzo libro delle Muse,* 5vv. (Gardano)

1569[19]   *Musica de' virtuosi della florida capella dell'illustrissimo et eccellent .. Duca di Baviera. Libro primo,* 5vv. (Scotto)

1569[20]   *La eletta di tutta la musica intitolata Corona* (Zorzi?)

1569[24]   *Di Filippo Azzaiolo bolognese il terzo libro delle villotte del fiore* (Gardano)

1570[14]   *Il secondo libro delle fiamme,* 5 and 6vv. (Scotto; = 1567[13])

1570[15]   *I dolci frutti, primo libro de vaghi et dilettevoli madrigali ... novamente posti in luce per il R.P.F. Cornelio Antonelli da Rimino detto il Turturino,* 5vv. (Scotto)

1570[16]   *Prima Stella. De madrigali a cinque voci, di Orlando Lasso, di Zanetto di Palestina. Di Giovan Nascho. Di Francesco Roscelli. Et altri. . .* (Scotto)

1570[18]   *Corona delle napolitane* 3 and 4vv. (Scotto)

1570[33]   *Il Turturino. Il primo libro delle napolitane ariose ... novamente per il Rever. P.E. Cornelio Antonelli da Rimino detto il Turturino acomodate sul leuto* (Scotto)

APPENDIX 2

PRINTS EDITED BY GIULIO BONAGIUNTA

1565[12]   *Il primo libro de canzone napolitane a tre voci ... di Giulio Bonagiunta da San Genesi* (Venezia: Scotto). Ded. to Gabriele Ottobon, 10/25/1565. Reprinted by Scotto (RISM 1567[18]).

1565[18]   *Le vive fiamme de' vaghi et dilettevoli madrigali dell'eccell. musico Cipriano Rore, a quattro et cinque voci, novamente posti in luce per Giulio Bonagiunta da S. Genesi* (Venezia: Scotto). Ded. to Annibale dal Forno, 11/8/1565. Reprinted by Scotto in 1569 (RISM R 2515), and by Scotto's heirs in 1576 (RISM R 2516) and 1585 (RISM R 2517).

L 786   *Orlandi Lassi ... quinque et sex vocibus ... sacrae cantiones nunc primum omni diligentia in lucem editae a Julio Bonagiunta ... Liber secundus* (Venezia: Scotto, 1565). Ded. to Domenico Paruta, abbot of San Gregorio, no ded. date.

1566[2]   *Primo libro de diversi autori a 4 voci. Intitulato Il desiderio. Novamente posti in luce per Giulio Bonagiunta da S. Genesi* (Venezia: Scotto). Ded. to Michel Trono, 11/24/1565.

1566[3]   *Il desiderio, secondo libro de madrigali a cinque voci ... novamente posti in luce, per Giulio Bonagiunta da S. Genesi* (Venezia: Scotto). Ded. to Alessandro Contarini, 12/5/1565.

1566[7]   *Canzone napolitane a tre voci. Secondo libro di Giulio Bonagiunta da S. Genesi* (Venezia: Scotto). Ded. to Marco Milano, Davit Grandonio, and Alvise Grimani, 11/20/1566.

1566[23]   *D'Hettor Vidue et d'Alessandro Striggio e d'altri eccellentissimi musici. Madrigali a 5 & 6 voci di novo posti in luce da Giulio Bonagiunta da S. Genesi* (Venezia: Rampazetto). Ded. to Giuseppe Grandonio and Camillo Trivisano, 6/1/1566.

1567[3]   *Primo libro de gli eterni mottetti di Orlando Lasso, Cipriano Rore, et d'altri ... a cinque et sei voci, di novo posti in luce per Giulio Bonagionta da San Genesi ... & con ogni diligentia corretti* (Venezia: Scotto). Ded. to Monsig. Sigismondo Borgaso, 7/22/1567.

1567[13]   *Secondo libro delle fiamme madrigali a 5 et 6 voci ... di novo posti in luce per Giulio Bonagionta da San Genesi ... & con ogni diligentia corretti* (Venezia: Scotto). Ded. to Antonio Villabruna da Feltre, 6/26/1567. Reprinted by Scotto (RISM 1570[14])

1567[16]   *Terzo libro del Desiderio. Madrigali a quattro voci ... Di novo posti in luce per Giulio Bonagionta da S. Genesi ... & con ogni diligentia corretti* (Venezia, Scotto). Ded. to Antonio Ronchale da Rovigo, 6/11/1567.

1567[23]   *Il cicalamento delle donne al bucato, et la caccia di Alessandro Striggio ... Di novo poste in luce per Giulio Bonagiunta da San Genesi ... & con ogni diligentia corretti* (Venezia: Scotto). Ded. to Giovanni Ferro da Macerata, 9/12/1567.

F 512   *Canzone alla napolitana a 5 voci ... [di] Giovan Ferretti, di novo poste in luce per Giulio Bonagionta da San Genesi ... et con ogni diligentia corrette* (Venezia: Scotto). Ded. to Benedetto Lazzarini, gentil huomo padovano, 11/7/1567.

1568[12]   *Il terzo libro delle fiamme. Madrigali a cinque voci de diversi eccellentissimi musici. Di novo posti in luce per Giulio Bonagiunta da S. Genesi ... & con ogni diligentia corretti* (Venezia: Scotto). Ded. to Genevra Salviati de' Baglioni, 4/22/1568.

1568[13]   *Gli amorosi concenti. Primo libro delli madrigali De diversi eccellentissimi musici a quattro voci, con un dialogo a otto ... Di novo posti in luce per Giulio Bonagiunta S. Genesi* (Venezia: Scotto). Ded. to Vito di Dorimbergo, 6/5/1568.

1568[16]   *Corona della morte dell'illustre signore, il sig. comendator Anibal Caro ... Di novo posta in luce per Giulio Bonagionta da S. Genesi* (Venezia: Scotto). Ded. to Giovanni Ferro da Macerata, 5/25/1568.

L 818   *Quintus liber concentuum sacrorum ... quinis, senis, octonis vocibus decantandis. Orlando de Lassus auctore, et Iulio Bonagiunta nunc primum in lucem edente* (Venezia: C. da Correggio). Ded. to Vincentio de Lucchis, bishop of Ancona, no ded. date.

1588[4]   (Doubtful) *Orlandi Lassi, Adriani Hawill, ac nonnullorum aliorum musicorum missae 4 & 5 vocibus decantandae, nunc primum a Giulio Bonaiuncta a S. Genesio in lucem editae. Liber primus* (Milano: Francesco & eredi S. Tini). No dedication.

The Dissemination of Pre-Corellian Duo and Trio Sonatas in Manuscript and Printed Sources: A Preliminary Report[*]

SANDRA MANGSEN

University of Western Ontario

In the Italian sources printed between 1600 and 1675 there are nearly 500 sonatas for two or three melodic instruments and approximately 1200 other duos and trios (*sinfonie, balletti, correnti*, etc.).[1] The period begins with Salamone Rossi's first book of trios (Venice, 1607) and concludes with the first decade of Giacomo Monti's publishing activities in Bologna. During these years, composers of instrumental music focused much of their attention on duos and trios rather than on the canzonas for larger ensembles more common early in the century or the solo sonatas that would achieve greater prominence later. Although the works in question provided the context, immediate and more removed, for Corelli's first published efforts, nowhere has there been an overview of the actual printed and manuscript sources in which this music was transmitted.[2] I propose here to give a preliminary report on my continuing investigation of the dissemination of this repertory in printed volumes and manuscript copies, and to take note of some concordances between them.

Eighty percent of the relevant prints were produced in Venice (by Vincenti or Magni) or in Bologna (by Monti); in general, they have survived three centuries relatively intact. Only two of the thirty-two instrumental volumes listed in Monti's catalogue from the 1680s have disappeared; for Vincenti, at least three-quarters of what is listed under "Canzoni per sonar a più voci" in the 1658 catalogue survives.[3] As for manuscript sources, relatively little of the instrumental repertory they transmit is independent of the printed sources (i.e., they are often copied from printed volumes), in marked contrast to the situation north of the Alps; nonetheless, manuscripts were critically important in the spread of instrumental duos and trios beyond Italy's borders, and of some significance for performance even within the country. [4]

Among the 112 printed sources initially examined for this study, there are volumes devoted primarily to vocal music that include only a few independent instrumental pieces, volumes of instrumental music mixing duos or trios with pieces for soloists or for larger ensembles, and many volumes that consist entirely of duos or trios. Although the specific terms *sonata da chiesa* and *sonata da camera* appear infrequently, repertories aimed primarily at sacred or secular uses can be differentiated on the basis of genre, instrumentation and texture.[5] This is not to say that individual pieces could not have served in more than one context, but that they were conceived primarily in terms of one function.

Before mid-century most prints containing instrumental duos and trios were devoted to music suitable for the church. By 1640, the larger churches in northern Italy ordinarily employed a "small number of singers with the support of one organ and strings (not winds)," and could import larger forces for special events. On such occasions even the smaller churches might hire a few extra singers and one or two violinists.[6] Thus, for volumes of concerted church music and sacred instrumental music that suited the personnel available in northern Italian churches, the market was apparently quite strong and stable.[7] The dance repertory for instrumental ensemble appeared in print more slowly than did the sacred, in part, no doubt, because a *corrente* was easier for an ensemble to improvise than was a *canzone*, so that the demand for printed dance music may have been less well developed than that for the church sonata. (In addition, some dance musicians may not have been formally trained, relying more on improvisation and memory than on fluency in reading notated parts). Dances for two or three instruments were published in large numbers only after the middle of the century, especially in the 1660s when volumes began to issue from Monti's press in Bologna. This printed repertory was addressed to all-purpose violinists who were capable not only of reading sonatas requiring the sixth position in church, but of playing dance music at court, or providing the instrumental music at meetings of the *accademie*. The dance, by this time, was no longer conceived simply *per ballare*, but also for the chamber filled with listeners. Sometimes the distinction is made clear in the prints, as in Bononcini's Op. 2 (1667d).[8]

One can make no particular assumption about the relation of date of composition and date of publication, other than the obvious one that the former precedes the latter. In some cases, compositions may have appeared in print shortly after they were written. Giovanni Maria Bononcini (1642–1678), for example, published so frequently during his twenties, that it is unlikely he had a large reserve of compositions. But his colleagues Giuseppe Colombi (1635–1694) and Giovanni Battista Vitali (1632–1692), who did not begin to publish until their thirties, may have had just such reserves. In any case, the date of publication is usually the only one available to attach to particular compositions.

This study will begin by describing the printed sources. When and by whom were they published? Which composers were most prominently represented? Is there any chronological, geographic, or other bias detectable in the printed repertory? The content of the prints will then be examined briefly with respect to genre, texture, and instrumentation. Having described the printed sources, we will turn our attention to manuscript concordances within and outside Italy, extending our chronological range as far as the beginning of the eighteenth century.

PRINTED SOURCES

The prints, the composers, and the publishers

Between 1600 and 1675 instrumental music was much less frequently printed than was either sacred or secular vocal music. A Vincenti catalogue from 1658 lists 808 volumes broadly categorized as sacred vocal, secular vocal, instrumental ensemble, theoretical or didactic, organ, and "music to sing or play with the flute or similar instruments."[9] Altogether there are 697 listings for vocal music and thirty-six for instrumental ensemble music.[10] Admittedly several of the vocal-music prints contain a few instrumental pieces, and a few of the composers represented in this catalogue only by their vocal music also published music for instruments (e.g., Marini, Legrenzi), but one must conclude from these listings that instrumental music was by far the loser in the race to the printing press. Indeed, of the twenty-four composers of instrumental volumes listed, fourteen are represented by their vocal music as well and three more are known from other sources to have published vocal music. In this context Bononcini's devotion to instrumental music becomes quite striking: his first nine publications (1666–1675) contained only music for instruments. And to have published only instrumental music, as Corelli did, was extremely unusual.

The fact that ninety percent of this repertory was the work of only thirty-three composers suggests that publication of instrumental music was available only to prominent individuals: indeed, most were *maestri di cappella* or organists in the major churches and cathedrals of northern Italy, often with powerful patrons on the secular side as well.[11] And within this elite group, some composers contributed a great deal more to the emerging duo and trio corpus than did others. Of those whose duos or trios appeared in print, more than half published fewer than ten such pieces. Although at least seventy-one individuals contributed to this printed repertory between 1600 and 1675, almost three-quarters of the extant duos and trios were written by only fourteen composers.[12] Thirty composers who published more than ten duos and trios before 1675 are listed in Table 1.

Most of those who paid scant attention to duos and trios were active early in the century, but many later composers continued to give such small ensembles only minimal attention, by including a few sonatas or canzonas in collections of sacred vocal music[13] or a few duos and trios in volumes intended primarily for four or more instrumentalists.[14] Among the composers who published only a few duos and trios were some well-known individuals (e.g., Cavalli, Rovetta, Banchieri), which confirms that instrumental music–at least the duo or trio–was not the most –obvious route to success in the seventeenth century.[15]

TABLE 1
A. Composers who published between eleven and thirty
duos or trios before 1675

Composer	Number of Volumes	Years of Publication	Number of Pieces
Arresti	2	1663–65	13
Castello	2	1621–29	22
Frescobaldi	1	1628	25
Fontana	1	1641	12
Gandini	1	1655	20
Grandi, O.	1	1628	12
Guerrieri	1	1673	16
Mazzaferrata	1	1674	12
Mussi	1	1620	16
Neri	2	1644–51	13
Pandolfi-Meali	1	1669	14
Pizzoni	1	1669	24
Polaroli	1	1673	22
Prattichista	1	1666	20
Prioli	1	1665	18
Riccio	2	1614–20	12
Rosenmüller	1	1667	11
Scarani	1	1630	18
Viviani	1	1673	12

Composers of between eleven and thirty printed duos and trios also span the period, but fully half of their volumes appeared between 1660 and 1675. The most productive composers (who published more than thirty duos and trios) had collectively authored fifty-six relevant volumes by 1675. Many of these individuals were born later in the century, and therefore grew up in a period when duos and trios already formed the common parlance, so that their propensity toward writing for the smaller ensemble is not surprising; however, several individuals had already made major contributions to this corpus by mid-century. Those who stand out for their early and significant contribution include Buonamente (d.1642), Cazzati (c.1620–1677), Marini (c.1587-1663), Merula (1594/5–1665), S. Rossi (1570–c.1630), Selma (fl.1638), and Uccellini (c.1603–1680).

As Table 2 demonstrates, both the number of composers whose duos and trios saw publication and the number of volumes they published varied only slightly from decade to decade, excepting a sharp decline that actually began in 1630, and a marked increase after 1665. Even the number of individual duos and trios varied little from decade to decade between 1626

TABLE 1 continued
B. Composers who published more than thirty duos
or trios before 1675

Composer	Number of Volumes	Years of Publication	Number of Pieces
Bononcini, G.M.	7	1666–75	120
Buonamente	4	1626–37	113
Cazzati	9	1642–70	177
Colombi	3	1668–74	38
degli Antonii, P.	2	1670–71	37
Falconiero	1	1650	46
Legrenzi	4	1655–73	69
Marini, B.	6	1617–55	125
Merula, T.	4	1628–51	74
Rossi, S.	4	1613–22	119
Selma	1	1638	35
Todeschini	1	1650	41
Uccellini	6	1639–67	191
Vitali, G.B.	4	1666–69	69

TABLE 2
Number of composers, printed volumes containing duos/trios, and
individual pieces by decade (1606–1675)

	06–15	16–25	26–35	36–45	46–55	56–65	66–75	Total
Composers	11	14	19	10	11	7	18	71
Volumes	11	15	18	13	12	13	30	112
Pieces	104	148	254	245	238	204	491	1684

and 1665.[16] Although it is not evident in an examination of the data by decade, the years between 1626 and 1630 were especially active ones; in the ensuing five years, little of any sort was published, due to the ravages of the plague in northern Italy.[17] In the final decade under consideration, more composers saw publication, often in multiple volumes, a development attributable in the main to Giacomo Monti's publishing efforts in Bologna.[18]

As the century progressed, the repertory for small ensemble was more and more likely to appear in homogeneous collections devoted solely to instrumental music (see Table 3) and exclusively to duos and trios. In the four decades between 1626 and 1665 the percentage of duo/trio volumes which included vocal music fell from half of those published to less than one-quarter. The same number of duos and trios was thus appearing in differently constituted volumes, devoted solely to instrumental music rather than mixed in content.

Even within the strictly instrumental collections, the proportion of duos and trios grew markedly after mid-century. Frescobaldi had systematically explored solo, duo, trio and quartet textures in his canzonas (1628i+j), as had Selma (1638c) and Fontana (1641b), Corradini (1624a) and

TABLE 3[a]
Character of printed volumes including instrumental
duos/trios by decade (1606–1675)

Character	Decade							
of Volume	06–15	16–25	26–35	36–45	46–55	56–65	66–75	Total
Instrumental	3	6	9	9	10	10	29	76
Inst-vocal	8	9	9	4	2	3	1	36

Montalbano (1629d). But between 1666 and 1675, ninety percent of the prints that included duos or trios emphasized those scorings; and in further contrast to earlier periods, only one of those volumes contained vocal music. By 1675, then, the emancipation of instrumental from vocal music, and the emergence of the duo and trio as the most common instrumental ensembles, were reflected clearly in the content and arrangement of the printed volumes.

That duos and trios formed an increasing proportion of the instrumental repertory in the years from 1620 to 1650 can be demonstrated not only from the content of extant volumes, but also from publisher's catalogues, independent of the peculiarities of what actually survives. In its only instrumental category, the Vincenti catalogue from 1621 lists twenty "Canzonette per sonar a più voci." Three-quarters of the volumes were advertised as containing pieces for four or more instruments.[19] By contrast, the 1649 catalogue lists thirty-two volumes: seven with pieces for four or six instruments; six with a variety of textures, including duos and trios; four confined to duos and trios; and one devoted to music for the bassoon, presumably in solo works.[20] (The content of the others cannot be determined from the catalogue.) Moreover, the seven volumes for four or more instruments were all holdovers from the earlier catalogue, representing stock still available; the new listings focused on solos, duos and trios.

Several different cities and publishing concerns brought this corpus into print, but of these only two cities and three firms were really important: Vincenti and Magni in Venice, and Monti in Bologna.[21] Table 4 compares the output of the major publishers from 1606 to 1675.

The Vincenti firm produced duo/trio volumes fairly consistently until 1645, although its production and share of the market were reduced between 1626 and 1635, when other publishers were actively contributing

TABLE 4
Number of duo-trio volumes per publisher by decade (1606–1675)[b]

Publisher	06–15	16–25	26–35	36–45	46–55	56–65	66–75	Total
Vincenti	8	8	6	7	3	1	1	34
Magni	1	7	7	5	7	9	7	43
Monti	0	0	0	0	0	0	16	16
Other	2	0	5	1	2	3	6	19
Total	11	15	18	13	12	13	30	112

to the duo/trio corpus. After 1645 the firm's production fell markedly; only fifteen percent of its duo/trio volumes belong to the last thirty years under consideration. But during those years, half of the extant duo/trio volumes were produced. Magni was important from 1616 to 1655, and dominated the market in the next decade. However, Magni's lessened output and the many volumes produced by Monti combined to weaken the firm's impact in the final ten years of the period.

Although the average number of duos/trios per volume does not differ significantly from one publisher to another,[22] Vincenti did print more volumes with just a few duos/trios than did Magni or Monti.[23] Chronology provides a partial explanation: Vincenti published more duos and trios in the first half of the century, when volumes of vocal music including one or two instrumental pieces were common; Monti, however, functioned only in the last third of the century, when instrumental publications devoted entirely to duos and trios had become the norm. All of the major publishers produced duos and trios in both vocal and instrumental volumes, but Monti's emphasis on the latter is quite striking, as is his production of twenty percent of all the instrumental volumes containing duos and trios within one decade (see Table 5). Of course this emphasis on instrumental music merely accords with the general publication practice for duos and trios in the decade when he became active. Monti certainly published vocal music: the one surviving catalogue contains eighty listings for vocal music and forty-one for instrumental.[24] Vincenti's 1662 catalogue by comparison has 148 listings for madrigals, 489 for sacred vocal music, and thirty-six for instrumental ensemble music as well as twenty-one organ intabulations, fourteen lute intabulations, nine theoretical works, and ninety listings of music to sing or play with chitarrone or similar instruments.[25]

Since the catalogues from Vincenti seem to represent whatever was on hand, rather than what was new, the case may be overstated, but to conclude that Monti was relatively more interested in instrumental music

TABLE 5
Character of volumes produced by major publishers[c]

Type of	Publisher				
Volume	Vincenti	Magni	Monti	Other	Total
Instrumental	19	30	15	12	76
Inst–vocal	15	13	1	7	36
Total	34	43	16	19	112

than was Vincenti seems reasonable enough. Moreover, Vincenti rarely made the few instrumental pieces in a collection obvious in its listings. In the five catalogues printed between 1621 and 1662, the presence or absence of the basso continuo and of instrumental parts in vocal music is often indicated, but the presence of independent pieces for instruments is not usually mentioned.[26] The apparent differences in emphasis on vocal and instrumental contexts for duos and trios seem at least as much a function of chronology as of publishers' attitudes: of Magni's seventeen duo/trio volumes after 1655, only two contained vocal music (1663a, 1665f). And Monti may have begun publishing instrumental music simply because he himself favored it over vocal, or because he saw a growing demand for such volumes. Whether he was influencing composers or responding to their concerns is rather difficult to determine, but one can have no doubt that instrumental music was flourishing in Bologna during the 1660s when Cazzati was *maestro di cappella* at San Petronio and Monti was just beginning to publish.

The practices of the major publishers differed somewhat with respect to the content of a typical volume. Vincenti's choices mimic quite closely the overall distribution of church sonata, dance and mixed publications.[27] Magni, with a larger total production of duo and trio volumes (forty-three vs thirty-four) published relatively more church sonata, fewer dance and more mixed volumes than the rival Vincenti firm. Monti and the other firms avoided mixed collections, and produced approximately equal numbers of church sonata and dance volumes. Thus, the publishers can be shown to have behaved differently in some respects; but their influence on composers is far from clear.[28]

Publishers reprinted their own and their rivals' volumes of duos and trios (see Table 6). Most of the reprints had no dedications and presumably did not directly benefit the composer. But beyond a possible payment to the composer, the costs of setting movable type for a reprint must have been comparable to those involved in the first edition;[29] perhaps the patron's main function in the case of a first edition was the provision of a subsidy in the face of the greater risk attached to initial publication.

The Italian style was spread to the north not only by individuals of Italian origin or training who found positions outside Italy, and by direct sales of Italian prints (evident in surviving collections such as those of the Sharp family and of Phillip Falle in England),[30] but also by foreign editions of Italian volumes, especially in Antwerp and (somewhat later) in London. Table 7 gives a partial list of such reprints of duo and trio volumes.

TABLE 6
Selected duo-trio volumes reprinted in Italy, 1620–90

Reprint	Composer	Publisher	First Edition	Remarks
1623a	Rossi	Vincenti	1613k Vincenti	first ed. lost
1624e	Turini	Vincenti	1621d Magni	expanded
1624f	Turini	Magni	1621d Magni	instrumental music only
1625d	Mussi	Vincenti	1620i Vincenti	
1627f	Bernardi	Vincenti	1621f Vincenti	
1628i*	Frescobaldi	Masotti	1628j Robletti	partial
1629e	Castello	Magni	1621n Magni	
1634	Frescobaldi	Vincenti	1628j Robletti	partial
1638h	Rossi	Vincenti	1613k Vincenti	first ed. lost
1639c	Merula	Vincenti	[1630] Vincenti?	first ed. lost
1641e	Rovetta	Magni	1626a Magni	
1642f	Rossi	Vincenti	1622b Vincenti	
1644e	Castello	Magni	1629f Magni	
1655d	Merula	Vincenti	?1630 Vincenti?	
1658a	Castello	Magni	1621n Magni	
1659a	Cazzati	Benacci	1656c Magni	
1659b	Cazzati	Magni	1648+ Magni?	first ed. lost
1663c	Cazzati	Dozza	1642e Magni	third printing
1664	Legrenzi	Magni	1663b Magni	
1668c	Vitali	Magni	1667e Monti	
1668f	Cazzati	Magni	1665a Silvani	
1670d	Vitali	Magni	1666a Silvani	
1671d	Vitali	Monti	1668e Monti	
1671a	Vitali	Monti	1667e Monti	
1671b	Legrenzi	Monti	1663b Magni	
1673k	Vitali	Monti	1668e Monti	
1674b	Bononcini	Monti	1671e Monti	new dedication
1677b	Bononcini	Magni	1673i Monti	
1677f	Bononcini	Monti	1673i Monti	

* The priority of these two editions is unclear

TABLE 6
continued

Reprint	Composer	Publisher	First Edition	Remarks
1677e	Bononcini	Monti	1672a Magni	
1677i	Vitali	Monti	1669f Monti	
1677h	Vitali	Magni	1668e Monti	
1677g	Vitali	Magni	1666a Silvani	
1677k	Legrenzi	Sala	1663b Magni	partial
1678e	Mazzaferrata	(Venice)	1674d Monti	
1678*	Mazzaferrata	Monti	1674d Monti	
1678d	Vitali	Monti	1668e Monti	
1679f	Viviani	Sala	1673b Magni	
1679c	Cazzati	Monti	1656c Magni	
1680b	Vitali	Monti	1666a Silvani	
1682g	Legrenzi	Sala	1673j Magni	
1682d	Vitali	Sala	1667e Monti	
1682f	Legrenzi	Sala	1656d Magni	
1685r	Vitali	Magni	1667e Monti	lost?
1688e	Mazzaferrata	Monti	1674d Monti	

* The two 1678 reprints of Mazzaferrata's Op.5 are not distinguished in RISM or Sartori. Copies in GB DRc and I Bc are from Venice (without publisher's name); that in GB LBl is from Bologna (Monti).

As early as 1651 with his publication of Cazzati's *Correnti e Balletti*, Phalèse in Antwerp seems to have been aware that Italian instrumental duos and trios were marketable. His reprinting in the 1650s of Castello's then thirty-year-old collection is striking, but not too surprising when one considers the number of thirty- or forty-year-old volumes Vincenti's catalogues continued to list and the fact that Magni too reprinted the Castello volumes at mid-century.[31] Sometimes even first editions appeared elsewhere. Carlo Farina went from Mantua to Dresden in 1625, where he was Konzertmeister at the Court until 1637. All of his music was printed in Dresden.[32] Both Cazzati's *Correnti e Balletti* (1651d) and Marini's *Corona Melodica* (1644c) may have been published first in Antwerp; Cazzati's collection was reprinted by Magni in Venice (1659b).[33]

TABLE 7
Selected volumes reprinted outside Italy, (1620–80)

Reprint	Composer	City: Publisher	First Edition
1621i	Belli	Frankfurt: Stein	1613b Magni
1651d	Cazzati	Antwerp: Phalèse	by 1648 Magni?
1656e	Castello	Antwerp: Phalèse	1629f Magni
1657d	Cazzati	Antwerp: Phalèse	1656c Magni
1658b	Castello	Antwerp: Phalèse	1621n Magni
1663d	Uccellini	Antwerp: Phalèse	1645f Vincenti
1668d	Vitali	Antwerp: Phalèse	1666a Silvani
1668h	Uccellini	Antwerp: Phalèse	1660d Magni, partial
1669d	Uccellini	Antwerp: Phalèse	c.1661 Magni
1674g	Cazzati	Antwerp: Phalèse	1656c Magni
1677j	Cazzati	Antwerp: Potter	1665a Silvani
1677d	Uccellini	Antwerp: Potter	c.1661 Magni

The average time before reprinting a volume for those listed in Tables 6 and 7 was ten years. The impression one has is of a fairly stable repertory, which continued to be played for at least a decade, and often for much longer. Rossi had been dead for more than ten years when Vincenti chose to reprint his last collection twenty years after its first appearance.[34] At the end of a long, if somewhat unstable career, Merula, an organist and violinist, had returned to Cremona in 1646, where he was still actively composing and publishing when Vincenti reprinted his Book 2 (1655d). That volume had appeared first c.1630–31, more evidence that a collection twenty-five years old was regarded as marketable in mid-century.

In selecting volumes to reprint, Italian publishers avoided composers who placed experimentation and originality foremost. Thus Biagio Marini, regarded today as one of the most interesting of the early composers for violin by both scholars and performers, apparently had no volumes reprinted in Italy.[35] Marco Uccellini, another composer who made higher than average technical demands on violinists, similarly had no Italian reprints, although several volumes were reprinted in Antwerp. Buonamente, whose secular publications were scored entirely for bowed strings and whose bass parts in particular were more demanding than was usual in secular music of the period, had no reprints at all. In contrast, Bononcini, Legrenzi, Rossi, and Vitali all provided music that was as functional as it was artistic

— and they were well-served by Italian publishers in terms of reprints, as were Castello and Cazzati. However, the latter two also had reprints in Antwerp, perhaps an indication that their sonatas in particular were appreciated far outside the context for which they were originally written. Bononcini and Vitali had no foreign reprints until Walsh found it profitable to issue their works in early eighteenth-century England, where the appetite for Italian music was nearly insatiable. Success, not only in the Italian market, but also in England, apparently required the skillful composition of works widely useful within the institutions that market served, but not straying too far beyond the customary technical demands and genre boundaries. Marini and Uccellini were not widely reprinted for the very reason that modern players and scholars have found their works interesting: they went far beyond what was usual.

Texture and instrumentation

The common terms *solo sonata* and *trio sonata* shelter a variety of textures treated individually by seventeenth-century composers and musicians: true solos (Sbc, Bb), duos (SSbc, SBbc), and trios of three melodic instruments with continuo (SSBbc).[36] Chronological trends, composers' idiosyncrasies, and differences in sacred and secular scoring practices help to explain this variation in textures and the development of the standard scoring practices represented in the trio sonatas of Corelli, en route to the eighteenth-century conception of the trio sonata for four instruments (SSBbc).[37] The treble-bass duo with continuo (SBbc) was most prominent early in the century in sonata/canzona collections. Toward the end of the period, the treble-bass duo appears in secular music, but often arises only as a result of *ad libitum* directions to omit inner parts. True solo sonatas, for one melodic instrument and chordal continuo (Sbc, Bbc), appeared less often than duos and trios: before 1670, only Puliti 1624l), Uccellini (1649b) and Leoni (1652b) had published collections entirely devoted to solo sonatas.[38] More often a few solos were included in a print devoted primarily to larger settings. The emergence after mid-century of entire volumes of pieces playable as violin solos (by omitting inner or melodic bass parts) illustrates within a strong duo/trio tradition the gradual development of the solo setting (Bononcini, 1673i; Cazzati, 1669a). Duos or trios for two treble instruments (SSbc, SSB and SSB/bc, the last with a bass partbook for *violone o spinetta*) were usually secular; only after mid-century did the treble-duo texture became common in the church sonata. Late in the period, volumes scored for two trebles with optional melodic bass (SS[B]bc) were common, evidence that the distinction between SS-Bbc trios an SSbc duos was beginning to evaporate in the church sonata of the 1660s. Nonetheless, the "standard" trio (SSBbc), for two trebles, melodic bass, and continuo, received attention from more composers and appeared in greater numbers than the duos, constituting thirty percent of the repertory over the entire period.

The repertory was intended in the main for instruments of the violin family. Eighty percent of the treble parts were meant for violin, as evidenced by labels employed in the sources. Only ten percent carry no information about instrumentation, and these come most often from the early part of the century. A miniscule number of treble parts exclude the violin completely (sixteen of 3028 examined); before 1630 cornetto was the most likely alternative. The 851 melodic bass parts studied carry less precise labels, but less than ten percent exclude a bowed string instrument. The bassoon and trombone were favored in Venetian prints early in the century, but are mentioned infrequently in later publications. Among the continuo instruments, the organ is associated with the church sonata, while the spinetta is mentioned most often in dance publications from the 1660s and 1670s, as alternative to the violone. The chitarrone and theorbo appear both as chordal continuo and as melodic bass instruments. The repertory as a whole is not particularly idiomatic or virtuosic, compared with works of Biber or Farina; those who made the most violinistic demands were the least likely to see their works reprinted (Marini, Uccellini). However we should note that the emerging solo repertory was more demanding than the duos and trios, as demonstrated by the four solo *sinfonie* of Montalbano (1629b).

Genre

In terms of genre, sonatas and *canzoni, balletti, correnti*, and *sinfonie* are most plentiful; other dances (*allemanda, brando, giga, gavotta, sarabanda*, and the instrumental *aria*) appear less frequently, and more erratically.[39] Over the seventy-five years, interest in the *canzone* and in the *gagliarda* declined, while the *allemanda, giga* and *sarabanda* became more popular. *Correnti* and *balletti* were published in increasing numbers as 1675 approached, but had long been part of the printed repertory. A typical volume was more likely to contain sonatas or canzonas than to focus exclusively on dances; volumes that did include dances were disproportionately associated with the most productive composers. While individual composers were more likely to publish church sonatas than sets of dances, the most productive typically contributed to both realms. But even the *correnti*, published throughout the period in substantial numbers, were produced by only nineteen of the seventy-one composers.

Career patterns help to explain certain choices. For example, the inclusion of French dance suites (*brandi*) in several publications of the 1660s is directly attributable to their composers' employment in Modena or in Parma at the Este and Farnese courts. Apparently, such suites are not to be found in Italian publications of composers without connections to these two courts.[40] Bononcini (1666c, 1667d, 1669g), Colombi (1668a), and Vitali (1667f) were all in Modena when their *brandi alla francese* were printed; Uccellini (1667g) had already moved to Parma from Modena. Indeed, the latter published no more church sonatas after moving from Modena to Parma. In Modena he had been *maestro di cappella* at the cathedral (1647–1665) and directed the instrumentalists at court until 1662; in Parma, however, he had no responsibility for sacred music, simply directing music at the Farnese court from 1665 to 1680. His last two instrumental publications contain only sinfonias à 2 or 3 and dances à 4, compositions presumably used in the operas and ballets he wrote for the courts.[41]

Summary

The Italian printed sources of the instrumental duo and trio repertory are fairly plentiful, and representative of what was originally published. For most of the period from 1600 to 1675, they constituted only a small percentage of the entire printed musical corpus and were produced by a correspondingly small number of composers. An even smaller group was responsible for the lion's share of this printed instrumental repertory. Some well-known composers are not represented at all among these printed volumes: Claudio Monteverdi, Alessandro Grandi, Marc Antonio Cesti, all of whom wrote for instruments in their concerted vocal music, however, and may thus have influenced composers of instrumental music indirectly.[42] Vincenti and Magni (in Venice), and Monti (in Bologna) were the major publishers, Vincenti primarily in the first half of the century and Monti only beginning in the 1660s. Between 1600 and 1675 duos and trios became more and more likely to appear in volumes devoted entirely to instrumental music and often scored throughout for two or three instruments; Monti was especially important for his emphasis on such homogeneous volumes. Many published volumes remained in the marketable repertory for ten or more years. The increasing publication of duos and trios and especially the reprinting of the most popular collections served to stabilize the repertory in Italy and contributed to the spread of Italian stylistic conventions northward. By 1675 the instrumental duo and trio had become a prominent feature of the musical scene, and these volumes were more and more likely to contain not only church sonatas, but dances, ordinarily to be played on instruments of the violin family. The groundwork for the eighteenth-century trio sonata had been laid in prints appearing by 1675.

Nevertheless, it is well to bear in mind that this printed corpus may represent only a fraction of the instrumental music originally written for small ensembles, and that notated music, in turn, a fraction of all the instrumental music heard in the seventeenth-century church, chamber, and theater. Manuscript distribution and improvisation must have played some role in the growth of an idiomatic instrumental style, but even the size of the printed vs. the hypothetical manuscript repertory cannot be reliably estimated, at least until more complete catalogues of sevententh-century manuscript sources are available. Improvisation leaves even fewer traces, but notation cannot be assumed to have played a role equivalent to the one it plays in today's art music. The relation of notation to performed dance music in the seventeenth century was probably more like that in rock music or jazz today: some players can read, others cannot; much of what one hears is improvised. There is some evidence that dance musicians played composed music from memory, but dances must also have been invented by the players in performance; certainly the dance improvised over a ground bass already had a long history by 1600.[43]

MANUSCRIPT SOURCES

While manuscripts in many repertories preserve works not found in any print, or pre-date printed versions of individual works (for example composing scores or fair copies made by a composer for the printer), copies of seventeenth-century Italian duos and trios most often derive from prints. Copies of printed works by Bononcini, Cazzati, Legrenzi, Vitali, and others have been noted in manuscript sources in Italy, France and England.[44] In the Estense collection in Modena, however, several of the manuscript volumes devoted to the works of local composers seem to lack concordances in printed volumes.[45] Alessandro Stradella offers perhaps the single most significant example of an important composer whose instrumental works were transmitted mainly in manuscript; others include such infrequently published composers as Lelio Colista (1629–1680), like Stradella, a Roman. [46]

Manuscript copies may have been produced after publication for a variety of reasons: to provide working parts in order to conserve library copies, to provide extra sets of parts, to adapt a piece to the particular occasion or to the actual performing forces available, to acquire a copy of an out-of-print volume, to acquire only a few pieces from a large published volume.

The existence of manuscript copies (in parts) of published works and the absence of performance markings in a large proportion of the trio sonata prints suggests that many were originally purchased as library copies, although enough manuscript annotations do occur to ensure that some volumes were actually used by performers.[47] In a few cases manuscript copies must have been essential because of the format of the printed copy, for example when four-part ensemble canzonas were issued in score (1624a).[48]

Major collections

1. Modena, Biblioteca Estense

Many of the manuscripts in the Estense collection in Modena seem to be fairly accurate copies of entire printed volumes. Most often the manuscripts seem to have been bound before copying, with each partbook contained in one gathering of several folios, and are copied in the same hand throughout. For instance the manuscript version of Vitali's Op. 1 (1666a) consists of three partbooks (*violino primo, violino secondo, violone*);[49] the first violin partook is made up of only one gathering of six bifolios; the music fills all of these pages, one dance per page presented in the same order as they are found in the print. Manuscript versions of Op. 2 (1667e), in three partbooks (*violino primo, violino secondo, organo*) and Op. 4 (1668e) are similarly structured: single gatherings, with content presented in the order found in the print, and with very little blank space. The latter, in the same hand as the Op. 2 manuscript, again consists of three partbooks (two violins and *violone o spinetta*) with no mention of the printed partbook's designation of the second violin as *ad libitum*.

Especially in the case of individuals employed at the Este court, one might imagine that these were the fair copies given to printers, since all present readings very close to those found in the printed volumes, even including the figured bass. However occasional omissions and outright errors do occur, suggesting that these manuscripts were copied from the prints rather than vice versa. Moreover, several similar manuscript copies of entire collections reduce the scoring compared with that in the prints. Copies of Bononcini's Op. 3 (1669g), Op. 5 (1671f), and Op. 7 (1673i), and of Vitali's Op. 3 (1667f), Op. 5 (1669f), and Op. 12 (1685j) all stem from the prints, but alter the scoring by omitting one or two viola parts. Presumably, the printers had worked from manuscript scores or parts no longer extant.

There are in addition several volumes devoted to manuscript works of Colombi, some of which include concordances to his printed volumes (e.g, Libro 11 and 12 contain several dances that appeared in the chamber sonatas of his Op. 5, 1689g), but others of which seem to transmit pieces he never published. Some of these are constructed as described above–single gatherings bound before copying, with pages completely filled. Libro 8, 9, and 11 are of this type. Other manuscripts seem to result from a later binding of previously copied parts: the evidence includes a variety of hands, the gathering structure, and peculiar aspects of the bass partbooks. The structure of Colombi's Libro 2 (Mus.F.272), apparently without significant concordances to his printed music, suggests that the originally separate folios were used by composer and performers, and later bound into one volume.

Of the concordances to published volumes, Colombi's Op. 2 (1673a), a collection of church sonatas, contains a rather odd selection of separate bass parts, now bound in one partbook: some have figures, others do not; some begin with an organ intabulation; some are transmitted in two versions, apparently melodic and chordal continuo parts.[50] In addition there are blank sides separating some of the sonatas, unlikely if the partbook had been bound before copying. The originally separate performing parts for each sonata were later bound together to form partbooks for the entire collection; Op. 3 (1674c) is similarly a later binding of separate parts, written on folios of varying sizes. The same composer's Op. 4 (1676b) also consists of originally separate folios, now bound together in three partbooks (two violins and bass); the print (1676b) has four (two violins, *bassetto viola*, and *basso continuo*). In the printed version, the melodic bass part is ordinarily busier than the continuo part; in the manuscript, the bass partbook follows neither *bassetto viola* nor continuo part exactly, but has elements of both, even within some individual sonatas. And Sonata 3 in the manuscript has duplicate bass parts–one much more virtuosic than the other, notated on opposite sides of one sheet, so that they cannot have been used simultaneously, but must have been alternates, perhaps for the older and larger *violone* and the smaller *bassetto* viola or violoncello.[51]

These manuscripts from the Este court form probably the largest collection of Italian manuscript sources for the duo-trio repertory of the 1660s and 1670s. Although those that are copies of prints differ very little from their models, they offer an opportunity to study at close hand the transmission and preservation of a repertory in one court about which a great deal is already known.[52] Manuscripts whose concordances with printed volumes have been identified in the library's catalogue are listed in Table 8.

TABLE 8
Manuscript concordances to printed volumes
in the Biblioteca Estense[d]

Composer	Volume	Manuscript Shelf No.	Print[87] Shelf No.
Bononcini	Op.1 (1666c)	Mus.F.105	
	Op.2 (1667d)	Mus.F.106	
	Op.3 (1669g)	Mus.F.107	
	Op.4 (1671e)	Mus.F.108	
	Op.5 (1671f)	Mus.F.109	
	Op.6 (1672a)	Mus.E.21	
	Op.7 (1673i)	Mus.F.110	
	Op.9 (1675b)	Mus.F.112	Mus.F.111
	Op.12 (1678a)	Mus.F.113	Mus.F.114
Colombi	Op.1 (1668a)	Mus.F.288	Mus.F.292
	Op.2 (1673a)	Mus.F.289	Mus.F.293
	Op.3 (1674c)	Mus.F.290	Mus.F.294
	Op.4 (1676b)	Mus.F.291	Mus.F.295
Corelli	Op.1–4 (1681–)	Mus.G.62	
	Op.2 (1685a)	Mus.F.36	Mus.F.306

2. The Rost Codex

The Rost manuscript is a collection of seventeenth-century chamber music copied by François Rost (d.1696), a priest who had musical duties at churches in Baden and then in Strasbourg; between 1680 and 1696 it is now held in Paris at the Bibliothèque nationale.[53] Its three partbooks contain about 150 pieces, primarily for two violins and organ continuo. Its composers are German and Italian, many of them associated with Vienna; Sebastien de Brossard acquired the collection in the late seventeenth century, whence it made its way to the Bibliothèque royal (predecessor of the Bibliothèque nationale) in 1726. Of the works with published concordances, none has been found to date after 1680, although the copying may have continued into the early 1690s. In addition to concordances in northern European prints and manuscript sources, its cataloguer has identified several concordances in Italian prints: Cazzati Op. 2 (1642e, 1), Op. 18

TABLE 8
continued

Composer	Volume	Manuscript Shelf No.	Print Shelf No.
Gaspardini	Op.1 (1683g)	Mus.F.476	Mus.F.475
Marini, C.	Op.1 (1687i)	Mus.G.123	Mus.F.694
Mazzaferrata	Op.5 (1674d)	Mus.E.128	
Torelli	Op.2 (1686d)	Mus.F.1179	Mus.E.232
	Op.3 (1687c)	Mus.F.1180	Mus.F.1178
	Op.4 (1687+)	Mus.E.231	
Vitali	Op.1 (1666a)	Mus.F.1240	Mus.F.1251
	Op.2 (1667e)	Mus.F.1247	Mus.F.1255
	Op.3 (1667f)	Mus.F.1241	Mus.F.1252
	Op.4 (1668e)	Mus.F.1242	Mus.F.1259
	Op.5 (1669f)	Mus.F.1248	Mus.F.1256
	Op.7 (1682c)	Mus.F.1243	Mus.D.531
	Op.8 (1683e)	Mus.F.1244	MuS.F.1253
	Op.9 (1684f)	Mus.F.1249	
	Op.11 (1684b)	Mus.F.1245	Mus.F.1254
	Op.12 (1685j)	Mus.F.1246	
	Op.13 (1689i)	Mus.D.532	Mus.D.530

Partial manuscript concordances to printed volumes
in the Biblioteca Estense[e]

Colombi	Op.5 (1689g)	Mus.G.60	(Libro 11)
	Op.5 (1689g)	Mus.F.281	(Libro 12)

(1656c, 13), Op. 22 (1660a, 3), Op. 35 (1665a, 1); Merula Op. 12 (1637a, 6); Rosenmüller (1667h, 3); Uccellini Op. 4 (1645f, 3) and Op. 5 (1649b, 1); and Vitali Op. 2 (1667e, 4).[54] One sonata from the Silvani anthology (1680a, where it is attributed to N. N. Romano) was also copied by Rost.[55] Many of the works in the manuscript are unattributed or carry attributions that conflict with those in other sources.

3. Selected English sources

The Rost manuscript shares several pieces in common with important English sources of Italian duos and trios, held in the British Library, the Bodleian Library, and the Durham Cathedral Library. The concordances with Italian prints that have thus far been identified are listed in Table 9.[56]

What strikes one as odd in these manuscript sources is the copying of only one sonata from an entire collection, as in several of the instances cited in Table 9. Was the volume/manuscript source available to the copyist for only a short time, or was this one sonata deemed the only piece worthy of the effort? Even if the manuscript at hand derived not from the print but from another manuscript source, a copyist at some point made the decision to include only one sonata from an entire print.

There was of course much more Italian music abroad in England than what is listed in Table 9.[57] In the manuscripts cited, and in others not yet examined for concordances to Italian prints, there are bound to be more sonatas and dances by Italian composers.[58] We should note as well that these manuscript sources, especially those held in the British Library and in Oxford, are not necessarily independent, since they share many of the same pieces, often presented in nearly the same order. Many of these manuscript copies derive immediately or at some remove from volumes imported into England directly from Italy or as reprints from publishers in France and the Low Countries.[59] Indeed, with the exception of Legrenzi's Op. 2 (1656d), English libraries even today hold copies of each of the prints (in first or later editions) from which the manuscript copies cited ultimately derived. Many of these extant copies belonged to identifiable English collections preserved from the late seventeenth or early eighteenth century.

Three English collectors around the turn of the century may serve as illustrations: Philip Falle (1656–1722), Edward Finch (1664–1738), and John Sharp I (1645–1714). Holograph catalogues of both Falle's collection and that of three generations of the Sharp family (which includes the Finch material) survive in Durham cathedral Library.[60] Falle's collection, much of it probably acquired on trips to the Low Countries in the service of William III, includes Italian and Dutch prints of music by Albinoni, Bononcini, Corelli, Castello, Mazzaferrata, Merula, Uccellini, Vitali, and others. John Sharp III (1723–1792), in the second half of the eighteenth century, owned manuscripts of music by Stradella, Ziani, Corelli, and Geminiani, as well as prints of Italian music by some of the same composers. His father (Thomas Sharp I, 1693–1758) had acquired some of this Italian material after the death of Edward Finch in 1738. That these

TABLE 9
Some concording printed and manuscript sources
in 3 English libraries

Composer	Printed Volume	Manuscript	Content
Anthology (Silvani)	1680a	Add.31436	11 sonatas
		Ms.Mus.Sch.d.254	no.7(Bononcini)
Bononcini, G.M.	Op.12 1678b	Ms.Mus.Sch.d.250	all, some transposed
Cazzati	Op.2 1642e	Ms.Mus.Sch.d.249	no.5
	Op.18 1656c	Ms.Mus.Sch.c.80	nos.1–5,7–12, capriccio
		Add.31431	nos.2–4,7–9,12
Legrenzi	Op.2 1655c	Ms.Mus.Sch.d.249	nos.2,3,11,12,15,18
		Add.31431	no.17
	Op.4 1656d	Ms.Mus.Sch.d.249	nos.1,3,5,7,8;6 Cor
	Op.8 1663b	Ms.Mus.Sch.d.254	no.1
		Ms.Mus.Sch.e.400–3	no.1
		Add.11588	nos.1,8
	Op.10 1673j	Add.31435	nos.4-6
Mazzaferrata	Op.5 1674d	Ms.Mus.Sch.d.260	no.3
Merula	Bk 2 1639c	Ms.Mus.Sch.d.249	no.8
Vitali	Op.1 1666a	Ms.M179–180	Bal 4,1,9; Cor 5,1,3
	Op.2 1667e	Ms.Mus.Sch.d.257	complete
		Add.31431	nos.4,8
	Op.4 1668e	Ms.M179–180	nos.1–16,18,20
	Op.5 1669f	Add.31431	nos.1,3,5
	Op.9 1684f	Add.31436	nos.2–8,11–12
		Ms.Mus.Sch.d.260	no.11
Viviani	Op.1 1673b	Ms.Mus.Sch.d.249	no.3

Manuscripts cited.
London, British Library: Add.11588, 31431, 31435, 31436
Oxford, Bodleian Library: Ms.Mus.Sch. c.80, d.249, d.254,
                                            d.257, d.260, e.400–3
Durham, Cathedral Library: Ms. M179–180

collectors, all ordained Anglican priests, acquired a great deal of English and Italian music that is both secular and instrumental is certainly of interest.[61] It was surely not the demands of their occupations, but their leisure interests, that led to these acquisitions, and encouraged some to expend significant time or money in obtaining copies of material not otherwise available.

A few Englishmen took their love of Italian music beyond collecting and performing by attempting to compose music in the Italian style. Thus Edward Finch not only copied much Italian music, but also left eleven of his own sonatas in his personal music book, dated 1717–20, three of which are found, later in the same manuscript, in versions "alter'd" by one Lorenzo Bocchi, dated October 1720.[62] Bocchi had presumably been engaged as a composition instructor, at least on a casual basis. Another English amateur, James Sherard (1666–1738), by profession an apothecary and by avocation a botanist and composer, actually published two collections of sonatas in imitation of Italian masters, confessing in the preface to the first that his access to Italian music was provided in volumes brought home by his brother, the botanist William Sherard.[63]

4. Düben and Leichtenstein-Castlecorn Collections

Two other large manuscript collections examined in the course of this study proved disappointing in their lack of Italian instrumental music derived from the Italian duo and trio prints: the Düben Collection in Uppsala and the Leichtenstein-Castlecorn collection in Kroměříž. The Düben collection contains complete manuscript copies of Corelli's Op. 4 (1694a) and 5 (1700a), as well as single sonatas from Op. 1 (1685a) and 5; there are also isolated instrumental pieces attributed to Albrici, Bertali, Buonamente, Melani, Valentini, T. Vitali, and Ziani. Many of the copies are dated from the 1650s to the 1670s; however, among the 300 instrumental works in the collection, there are few if any concordances with the prints examined in the first part of this essay. Most of the composers represented in the collection were Austrian, or active in German-speaking lands: Schmelzer is particularly prominent. Nonetheless, in the two years before she abdicated (in 1654), converted to Catholicism, and left Stockholm to reside in Rome, Queen Christina had maintained a group of Italian musicians at her court. Vincenzo Albrici (1631–1696) was the leader of those musicians from November 1652 until June 1654. Albrici, born in Rome, and not represented in the Italian published duo and trio repertory, left several concerted pieces and a few for instruments in the Düben collection, although Kjellberg asserts that much of it may date from after his departure from Stockholm.[64] (The Italian troupe was disbanded after Christina's departure.) Other Italians represented in the collection by their concerted music include Monteverdi, Bontempi, Bernabei, Carissimi, and Cazzati. In fact the list of Italian-composed vocal music, including motets, madrigals, arias, and cantatas, is quite long–over 100 names are found. Some of these composers of the seventeenth and eighteenth centuries were also important to the development of few-voiced instrumental music: Viviani, Polaroli, Gratiani, and Legrenzi. It seems odd then to find them represented only by their vocal music, and especially odd in a Protestant country to find that Italian-composed motets outweigh seemingly more "neutral" instrumental music.[65]

The instrumental music in the Leichtenstein-Castelcorn collection in Kroměříž has been described by Ernst Hermann Meyer and by Jiří Sehnal.[66] Works by 122 composers are contained in this collection, some of whom were employed by Karl Leichtenstein-Castlecorn, Prince-Bishop of Olomouc from 1664 to 1695, when as many as thirty-eight instrumentalists played in the orchestra at court.[67] Biber was the Kapellmeister until 1670, and many of his compositions are found in the collection. Most of the composers represented here had close ties to Leopold I in Vienna, but many works are unattributed, so that a search for concordances between these manuscripts and the Italian printed repertory seemed worthwhile. However, no concording sources for sonatas in the Italian printed repertory have yet been found. Among the Italians who do appear, Alessandro Poglietti is represented by several ensemble sonatas in manuscript, which were never published in Italy; he worked in Vienna from 1661 until his death in 1683. Among the few printed volumes is a reprint from the 1690s of a collection first published in Freiburg (c.1667) that contains twenty sonatas by Pietro Andrea Ziani for three to six instruments; the collection had been partially reprinted in Italy in 1678.[68] Ziani (1616–1684) had spent his early career in Venice and Bergamo, but by 1662 was in Innsbruck, and then in Vienna as Vice-Kappellmeister to the Dowager Empress Eleonora. By 1669 he was back in Venice as first organist at San Marco; after 1677 he worked in Naples. His sonatas, like those of Poglietti, are presumably in this collection because of his ties to the Austrian court.

Some further aspects of the manuscript concordances

1. Creation or reorganization of suites

Manuscript sources, when they do offer concordances with prints, often present readings that vary significantly from their exemplars, printed or manuscript. For example, a manuscript now in the Durham Cathedral Library (Ms. M179–180) presents (without attribution) and reorganizes into more coherent suites dances from Vitali's Op. 1 (1666a) and Op. 4 (1668e). Op.1 contains twelve *balletti*, followed by twelve *correnti*, not paired in any way. The manuscript source presents three *balletto-corrente* pairs.[69] Similarly, the original print of Op. 4 and a series of Italian reprints contain four *balletti* followed by a seemingly odd assortment of two- and three-dance groups, but the copyist of the Durham manuscript treats each *balletto* as the opening dance of a suite in the same key.[70]

2. Reductions of performing forces

Manuscript sources also seem to adapt instrumental and vocal pieces to suit the forces locally available, or perhaps simply to reflect the taste of the copyist. Thus in the Rost manuscript, ten pieces for which concording sources have been identified are reductions from larger settings preserved elsewhere, three of them in the Düben collection.[71]

Since many Italian prints incorporate *ad libitum* directions to omit inner or melodic bass parts, or to omit the ripieno voices or instruments,[72] it is no surprise to find similar reductive procedures in the Estense collection of Modenese manuscripts.[73] Bononcini Op. 5 (1671f) consists of dances for five or six strings; the manuscript source does not transmit the inner (viola) parts, and includes only four partbooks (two violins, *violone*, and *basso continuo*; similarly his Op. 3 (1669g) has three partbooks (two violins, *violone*) in manuscript, a reduction from the original four of the print; Op. 7 (1673i) has been reduced from four printed partbooks (with *ad libitum* directions for performance on one, two, three, or four instruments) to three manuscript partbooks without any *ad libitum* directions. The same pattern is characteristic of many of the manuscript copies of Vitali's printed collections: his Op. 3 (1677f) has four printed partbooks (*violino primo, violino secondo, alto viola*, and *spinetta o violone*, figured), but only three manuscript ones (*violino primo, violino secondo*, and *violone*, figured); his Op. 5 (1669f) has five partbooks in the print (*violino 1 and 2, viola, violone, organo*) and four in the manuscript (lacks viola); Op. 12 (1685j), à 5 in the print (2 violins, violas, *violone o spinetta*) is reduced to three partbooks in the manuscript (2 violins, and *basso o violone*). Thus, the Modena copyists seem determined to reduce any dances and sonatas for larger ensembles to trios, presumably a reflection of the standard performance of dances at that court. Elsewhere, as the printed versions demonstrate, larger ensembles may well have performed the same repertory.

3. Instrumentation

Often, Italian sonatas for violins were published in versions appropriate for recorders, especially in England. For instance, G. M. Bononcini's Op.12[74] was reprinted in two separate editions by Walsh in London, one in the original version for two violins and bass,[75] the other with twenty of the twenty-four dances transposed (and a few reordered as well) to make them suitable for recorders.[76] Walsh also added a part for the harpsichord figured only for the first few dances (the original Italian print was unfigured). And these dances are found in an English manuscript source as well (Ms.Mus.Sch.d.250), in the version suitable for recorders.[77]

Corelli's sonatas were also transmitted in manuscript copies. For instance, James Sherard owned a manuscript copy of Op. 2 (Ms. Mus. Sch. d.255) in four partbooks (two treble, *bass de viol*, and a figured bass); since the original had only three partbooks (2 violins, *violone o spinetta*), Sherard's two bass partbooks may represent an adaptation to northern or simply to later practice (also reflected in many Dutch reprints) of doubling the continuo line. Another English manuscript copy of Op. 2, owned by Thomas Britton (d.1714), similarly consists of four partbooks Ms.Mus Sch.c.76). Corelli's Op.5, which appeared in English prints transposed for recorder, also appears in a manuscript source in the Bodleian Library (Ms.Mus Sch.e.405), which contains the bass parts for eleven of the twelve sonatas (lacking No. 12, the Folia variations, and part of No. 9), four of them transposed down by a major second of perfect fourth, probably to make them more suitable for the recorder.[78]

****

The study of collections, both printed and manuscript, gives us some insight into the reception of Italian music at home and beyond Italy's borders. James Sherard, Edward Finch, John Sharp I, and Philip Falle all represent English musicians or amateur composers with an avid interest in Italian music. Sherard, for example, must have spent a great deal of time and money assembling his collection of Italian music, if we can judge by the extent of the manuscript sources somehow connected to him now held in the Bodleian Library. He himself is known to have copied works of Rosenmüller (Ms.Mus.Sch.d.248, eleven sonatas from the 1682 print), Lelio Colista (Ms.Mus.Sch.d.256, eleven sonatas, most of which are also found in Ms.Mus.Sch.e.400, and in Lbl Add.33236), twelve sonatas in Ms.Mus.Sch.d.254 (also found in Ms.Mus.Sch.e.400-3, including one by Bononcini, and one from Legrenzi's Op. 8), and other Italian works, in addition to having two sets of his own very Italianate trio sonatas published in Amsterdam (1701 and c.1711).[79] His interest in Italian music is amply confirmed by the extent of his collection and his activities as a composer. But only rarely are we so well informed about particular collectors or copyists.

Unless we know the actual route by which a copy came to be in someone's hands, the degree to which it resulted from a determined search or rather from happenstance, we cannot infer a great deal about the individual's taste.[80] Still, the degree to which collections are formed from particular segments of the repertory must be somewhat indicative of the collector's regard for the music itself. We know then that François Rost, whose copied parts may never have been used by performers, placed a high value on Italian sonatas;[81] and that in Uppsala and Olomouc, works by Italians "in residence" appear more often than do works by those who remained in Italy, demonstrating that personal association outweighed any more general thirst for Italian sonatas. And in England we can be sure from the extensive concordances of pre-1675 Italian music in manuscript sources that native musicians were well prepared to receive the sonatas of Corelli.

Corelli's Opera 1–4 appeared in 1681, 1685, 1689, and 1694, a span of fourteen years. The solo sonatas appeared in 1700, and the concerti grossi in 1714, after his death. Vitali and Bononcini were much quicker to see their works into print. Vitali published his first four volumes between 1666 and 1669; Bononcini's first five volumes appeared between 1666 and 1671. But Vitali and Bononcini were exceptional; the more usual rate of publication for active composers of instrumental music was that of degli Antonii (1670, 1671, 1676, 1686) or Colombi (1668, 1673, 1674, 1686, 1689).

Corelli was surely heavily indebted to his Bolognese mentors and associates, and to those in Rome, but the reception of his works as measured by the number of reprints far outweighs that of his contemporaries. Seven Italian reprints of Opus 1 had appeared by 1688, and these were followed by editions in Amsterdam, Antwerp, London and Paris, in addition to further Italian reprints. Yet exclusive concentration on Corelli inhibits the identification of other conduits through which seventeenth-century instrumental styles reached the composers of the eighteenth century. Giovanni Maria Bononcini died in 1678, but his son Giovanni (1674–1747) published six volumes of instrumental music in Bologna during the 1680s.[82] In the 1690s, when he lived in Rome, Naples, and then Vienna, Giovanni wrote mainly operas and cantatas.[83] Vitali's son, Tomaso Antonio Vitali (1663-1745), not only edited his father's final collection of dances for publication (1692d), but was himself an important composer of trio sonatas published in the 1690s. Thus, although Corelli may be the most visible Italian model for later composers, he was not the only seventeenth-century Italian composer whose instrumental music was widely circulated. It would surely be a mistake then to measure the sonata in the eighteenth century solely in terms of his legacy.

Endnotes

*   The various phases of this research have been supported by a Fulbright Scholar Award (1989–90), a research grant from the Social Science and Humanities Research Council of Canada (1990–91), and grants for the purchase of computer equipment and microfilms from the University of Western Ontario (1989–90 and 1990–91). I am grateful to Stephen Bonta and Lowell Lindgren for reading an earlier version of this paper.

1   Only volumes printed in Italy have been included in this survey. Thus Italian publications of Rosenmüller, a German resident in Venice, have been examined, while non-Italian publications of Italian expatriates like Farina have been excluded.

2   Christopher Hogwood devoted only a few pages to this repertory in his brief book on the trio sonata, but Willi Apel and Peter Allsop have now provided us with more extensive information on this large corpus of instrumental music. Christopher Hogwood, *The Trio sonata* (London: BBC Publications, 1979); Willi Apel, *Italian Violin Music of the Seventeenth Century*, ed. Thomas Binkley (Bloomington: Indiana University Press, 1990), trans. and enlarged from "Die italienische Violinmusik im 17. Jahrhundert," *Beihäfte zum Archiv für Musikwissenschaft* Bd.21 (Wiesbaden: Franz Steiner, 1983); Peter Allsop, *The Italian 'Trio' Sonata: From its Origins to Corelli* (Oxford: Clarendon Press, 1992). See also the series of articles in two issues of *Early Music* 18/4 (Nov. 1990) and 19/1 (Feb. 1991) stemming from the conference "The Italian Violin School to the time of Corelli," organized by Neal Zaslaw at the Boston Early Music Festival, 1987. Finally, my own dissertation deals at length with the printed sources of instrumental duos and trios: "Instrumental Duos and Trios in Printed Italian Sources, 1607–1675" (Ph.D. diss., Cornell University, 1989.)

3   Oscar Mischiati, *Indici, cataloghi, e avvisi degli editori e librai italiani dal 1591 al 1798* (Florence: Olschki, 1983), includes four Vincenti catalogues (Mischiati VII–X, spanning the period 1621–1662) and one from Monti (Mischiati XIII, c.1682).

4   The most extensive collection is in Modena, Biblioteca Estense, and contains works by Colombi, Vitali, Mazzaferrata, Bononcini, and others; many of these manuscript sources duplicate printed volumes held in the same library.

5   One effective way to separate sacred and secular repertories is according to the number of bass partbooks. Secular volumes ordinarily had only one, which may demand a chordal realization, or be reserved for a melodic instrument alone; sacred volumes often had both continuo and melodic bass partbooks, and mention the organ as chordal continuo instrument. It must be said that this distinction between sacred and secular practices begins to fade in the 1670s and in reprints of the repertory outside Italy. See my "Instrumental duos and trios," 446–48 and "The Trio Sonata in Pre-Corellian Prints: When does 3 = 4?" *Performance Practice Review* 3 (1990) 138–64.

6   See Jerome Roche, *North Italian Church Music in the Age of Monteverdi* (Oxford: Clarendon Press, 1984), 19. See also Stephen Bonta, "The Use of Instruments in Sacred Music in Italy 1560–1700," *Early Music* 18 (1990): 519–35 and Anne Schnoebelen, "The Role of the Violin in the Resurgence of the Mass in the 17th Century," *Early Music* 18 (1990): 537–42. According to Schnoebelen the trio texture of two trebles and continuo was central to mass composition before mid-century: "By the end of this decade [1630s] a typical combination for the *messa concertata* is five voices, both solo and tutti, and two violins plus continuo." Ibid., 540

7   On the function of instrumental music in the church services, see Stephen Bonta, "The Uses of the Sonata da Chiesa," *Journal of the American Musicological Society* 22 (1969): 54–84.

8   Citations of the form "1667d" refer to Claudio Sartori, *Bibliografia della Musica Strumentale Italiana stampata in Italia fino al 1700*, 2 vols. (Florence: Olschki, 1952, 1968). In Op.2 Bononcini designated twenty-six dances (for one, two, and three instruments) *da camera*, and the final ten (for three and four instruments) *in stil francese da ballo*.

9   "Indici di tutte le opere di musica che si trovano nella stampa della pigna di Alessandro Vincenti," in Mischiati, *Indici*, 187–212.

10   A single listing may include more than one volume, since a composer's first and second books may be grouped together.

11   For a discussion of the relation between a composer's occupation and his compositions, see Eleanor Selfridge-Field, "Instrumentation and Genre in Italian Music, 1600–1670," *Early Music* 19 (1991): 61–67.

12   Nineteen composers published between eleven and thirty pieces, and fourteen produced more than thirty. A fairly accurate list of all composers who published duos and trios before 1675 is in Table 1.1 of my "Instrumental Duos and Trios," 23–24.

13   Allevi (1668b), Cavalli (1656a), Filippi (1649d), and Medico (1665f); and similarly, in earlier volumes of Cecchino (1628e) and Cima (1610d).

14   Corradini (1624a) and Ferro (1649e).

15   The first two composers mentioned included a few duos and trios in volumes devoted primarily to sacred vocal music (1656a, 1626a); Banchieri's *Il virtuoso ritrovo academico* (1626) included six pieces for two to five instruments in a collection of secular vocal music. One was reprinted from an earlier volume but altered to suit a more secular context, i.e., the organ and trombone were replaced by harpsichord. See Warren Kirkendale, *L'Aria di Fiorenza* (Florence: Olschki, 1972)for an extensive discussion of this piece, and of instrumental and vocal settings of the same bass by other composers.

16   Between 1616 and 1665 printed duos and trios appeared at a relatively consistent rate, but the first and last decades depart significantly from the others: the number of pieces published in the final decade (1666–75) is over three times the number published between 1606 and 1615.

17   In fact all but two of the new volumes produced between 1626 and 1635 appeared before 1630. Tarquinio Merula's *Il secondo libro delle canzoni da suonare a tre*, Op.9, may have been printed in 1630 or 1631; it was reprinted (or perhaps finally printed) by Vincenti in 1639, and in 1655. The last edition was advertised in Vincenti's 1658 catalogue. The 1630/31 edition is lost, but the 1639 edition lacks a dedication, so it may well have been a reprint. A volume of sonatas by Scarani was produced in 1630, and Vincenti's reprint of the Frescobaldi canzoni is dated 1634. Otherwise Venetian music presses produced no instrumental ensemble music until 1635.

18   John G. Suess, "The Rise of the Emilian School of Instrumental Music in Late 17th-century Italy," *La Musique et le rite sacré et profane: Report of the Thirteenth Congress*, vol. 2, ed. Marc Honegger and Paul Prevost, *Report of the International Musicological Society Congress* 13 (1986): 507–8.

a   The character of the volume is instrumental if it contains only instrumental music, inst-vocal if it contains vocal and instrumental music. The contingency tables are included here as an efficient means of presenting a great deal of information. But in order to be certain that the two factors in the table interact in any meaningful way, the chi square (X^2) value for the table must be given as well. In general, the chi square is a test of the null hypothesis that the two parameters are statistically independent, or in this case that the probability of a volume's containing a piece in a given genre is not affected by the decade, and vice versa. The larger the chi square, the more likely that the null hypothesis should be rejected and that chronology did affect content of these volumes. The number of degrees of freedom is derived from the number of rows and columns in the table, and helps to determine the level of confidence for the chi square statistic. The level of confidence for Tables 3–5 is 95% or higher unless otherwise noted. For Table 3, $X^2 = 29.51$ with 6 degrees of freedom.

19   Mischiati, *Indici*, 135–53. Of the others, one was devoted entirely to duos, one did not specify ensemble size, and the other two contained pieces for ensembles of several different sizes.

20   Ibid., 163–86.

21   Vincenti was in partnership with Ricciardo Amadino from 1583 to 1586; after 1586, Vincenti used his own printer's mark, but the two firms shared type faces, ornaments and decorative initials. Having apprenticed to Gardano, Bartolomeo Magni inherited that firm in 1611. The Gardano name was retained on prints through 1651, when Francesco Magni began to sign them. See Claudio Sartori, *Dizionario degli editori musicali italiani: tipografi, incisori, librai-editori* (Florence: Olschki, 1958), 6–7 and 91-93. These firms are treated as units Amadino/Vincenti and Gardano/Magni in the analyses that follow.

b   For Table 4, $X^2=78.66$ with 18 degrees of freedom.

22   Among the three major publishers and the others as a group, the average number of duos and trios per volume is fifteen.

23   Half of the volumes produced by other publishers included fewer than six duos or trios; for Vincenti that figure rises to ten; for Magni twelve, and for Monti fifteen.

c   For Table 5, $X^2=7.418$ with 3 degrees of freedom. (This X^2 just fails to reach the .05 level of significance, in this case 7.81.)

24   Mischiati, *Indici*, 264–70.

25   *Ibid.*, 213–41.

26   In the 1649 catalogue (Mischiati, 163–86), Carlo Milanuzi's *Armonia Sacra* (No. 293) and Giacomo Ganassi's collection of motets (No. 511) were listed as including canzoni; Tomaso Cecchino's volume (No. 417) was said to contain twenty-two motets and eleven sonatas. But these were clearly exceptional listings. Riccio's *Il secondo libro delle divine lodi accommodate per concertare nell'organo ... con alcune canzoni da sonare a duoi & a quattro stromenti* (1614g) contains seven instrumental pieces. Following the more usual pattern, it was listed in the 1621 catalogue (Mischiati, 135–53) along with his first book as, "Divine laudi Riccio a 2; Idem secondo a 2, 3, 4, 5 con messa a 2" (Nos. 254–55).

27   Table A5 in my "Instrumental duos and trios," 467, gives the actual figures for each publisher.

28   The observed differences between publishers are confined to the specific areas mentioned; there are no overall differences that hold up under statistical analysis in the genre content of volumes put out by the various publishers. Thus, individual publishers cannot be shown to have exerted wide-ranging influence over the nature of the published repertory of duos and trios. This is not to suggest that publishers had no influence over volume content — but merely that they seem to have been more or less in agreement about the proper content of volumes printed.

29   Setting type was a highly labor-intensive activity. Eleanor Selfridge-Field reports that the "minimum rate of type-setting stipulated by Venetian law was half a folio a day." Thus Marini's Op. 8 at 72 folios could have required as much as 144 days for one type-setter to produce. See Eleanor Selfridge-Field, "Dario Castello: A non-existent biography," *Music & Letters* 53 (1972): 179–80, n.1.

30   Holograph catalogues of these collections are in the Durham Cathedral Library: Falle, Add.ms.154 and Sharp, Ms.M194, respectively. For more information about these three individuals and their collections, see the introductions to the printed catalogues. R. Alec Harman, A *Catalogue of the Printed Music and Books on Music in Durham Cathedral Library* (London: Oxford University Press, 1968); Brian Crosby, *A Catalogue of Durham Cathedral Music Manuscripts* (London: Oxford University Press, 1986).

31   Castello's works were still being copied in manuscript as late as the 1670s along with those of composers a generation younger. *The New Grove Dictionary of Music and Musicians*, s.v. "Castello, Dario." Castello's biography has been difficult to trace; his association wih San Marco is documented only by title page information on prints from Venice and Antwerp. See Selfridge-Field, "Dario Castello," 179–90.

32   *The New Grove Dictionary of Music and Musicians*, s.v. "Farina, Carlo."

33   Since the Antwerp print of Cazzati's Opus 4 has no dedication and appeared only in 1651, it was undoubtedly a reprint of an earlier Italian edition, printed in Venice between Opus 2 (Magni, 1642e) and Opus 8 (Vincenti, 1648). There is no guarantee that the original edition was the work of Magni, since he was a frequent borrower, but it is probable since the Vincenti catalogues do not advertise the volume. On similar but less compelling grounds doubts might be raised about the initial printing of the Marini volumes except that he was outside of Italy for some of the time between 1623 and 1649, in Brussels, Düsseldorf, and elsewhere. Moreover the volume is dedicated to Anna Catharina Constantiae Serenessimorum Poloniae. *The New Grove Dictionary of Music and Musicians,* s.v. "Marini, Biagio."

34   The Venetian copyright protected first editions for twenty years, later editions for ten years in Venice and elsewhere. Selfridge-Field, "Dario Castello," 180, n.2.

35   These assertions about reprints are based on the extant sources rather than on a study of publishers' catalogues or other contemporary evidence. But there is no particular reason to assume that Marini's hypothetical Italian reprints would have been less likely to have survived than the reprints of volumes by other composers.

36   Other duo and trio textures, encountered much less frequently, include SSSbc, STBbc, and BBbc. This abbreviated terminology is adapted from William S. Newman, *The Sonata in the Baroque Era*, 4th ed. (New York: Norton, 1983). In my usage, capital letters refer to melodic instruments; bc to chordal continuo alone.

37   See my discussion of the role of the bass instruments in "The Trio Sonata in Pre-Corellian Prints."

38   For Uccellini, see Fred Pajerski, "Marco Uccellini (1610–1680) and his Music" (Ph.D. diss., New York University, 1979). Pajerski includes eight complete solo sonatas of Uccellini, in facsimiles of the continuo part, from Opus 5 (1649b) and Opus 7 (1660d).

39   For a more detailed treatment of this topic, see Chapter 2 and Tables A2 and A3 (461–65) in my "Instrumental Duos and Trios."

40   Cazzati's Op.22 (1660a) and Op.30 (1662) each contain two dances labelled *brando* but these are single binary movements, rather than suites.

41   Upon the death of Duke Alfonso IV in 1662, his widow (Mazarin's niece) dissolved the court chapel in Modena, so that Uccellini had only his position at the Duomo until he went to Parma. His Opus 8 (devoted to sinfonias) was first printed c. 1661, before the dissolution of the court chapel. Opus 9 was printed two years after he went to Parma. Pajerski, "Marco Uccellini," 50–51 and 106.

42   Selfridge-Field, *Venetian Instrumental Music from Gabrieli to Vivaldi* (Oxford: Blackwell, 1975), 119–24.

43   Peter Holman has suggested that sixteenth-century "dance musicians, in common with other professional instrumentalists, did not use written music, so they must have played a composed repertoire from memory." *Four and Twenty Fiddlers: The Violin at the English Court 1540–1690,*(Oxford: Clarendon Press, 1993), 30. In a similar vein, one often sees speculation about the lack of compositions for organ by well-known virtuosi, who may have left no notated compositions for their instrument simply because producing organ service music was still regarded as an improvisatory art, even its technique transmitted primarily through the oral tradition.

44   In the present phase of the study I have examined manuscript collections of seventeenth-century instrumental music in Sweden (Düben Collection in the Universitetsbiblioteket, Uppsala), Great Britain (collections in the Durham Cathedral Library, Bodleian Library, and the British Library), Italy (Biblioteca Estense) and Czechoslovakia (the Leichtenstein-Castlecorn collection in Kroměříž). For the Rost manuscript (Bibliothèque nationale Rés. Vm7 673), I have employed the thematic catalogue of M. Alexandra Eddy, *The Rost Manuscript of Seventeenth-Century Chamber Music: A Thematic Catalog* (Warren, Michigan: Harmonie Park Press, 1989).

45   Those without concordances to the printed sources are attributed in the main to Colombi.

46   See Carolyn Gianturco and Eleanor McCrickard, *Alessandro Stradella (1639–1682): A Thematic Catalogue of his Compositions* (Stuyvesant, NY: Pendragon, 1991); for Colista, see Eleanor McCrickard, "The Roman Repertory for Violin Before the Time of Corelli," *Early Music* 18 (1990): 563–73. Colista left about twenty-nine church trio sonatas; several of them are found in English sources: LB1 Add.33236; Ob Ms.Mus.Sch.e.400–403 and Ms.Mus.Sch.d.256. However, Peter Allsop has suggested that many of Colista's works in British manuscripts are actually by Lonati; see his "Problems of Ascription in the Roman Sinfonia of the Late Seventeenth Century: Colista and Lonati," *The Music Review* 50 (1989): 34–44.

47   The occasional survival of an "extra" printed continuo partbook in an already complete set leads to the suspicion that individuals may occasionally have purchased extra parts because of the possibilities of a particular performance milieu combined with an unwillingness to make manuscript copies. But the survival of such "extra" printed parts is rare. Similarly the survival of partial sets (e g., violin 1 and basso continuo, or only the inner parts) suggests that such subsets of published partbooks were needed for or

were irrelevant to particular performance milieux, and thus were taken or left behind as group. Of course some surviving incomplete sets of partbooks must result from mere happenstance.

48   Even when a publication appeared in parts, there may sometimes have been more per-formers than partbooks, demonstrating that the arrangement and number of partbooks is not always a clear cut indication of the number of performers necessary. Sometimes two performers shared one book, reading separate parts from facing pages (Uccellini: 1639b, 1642a). In at least one instance, Marini expected singer and violinist to share not only one book, but the very same part. In *Si quella bella bocca*, à 5, the singer is ad-vised: "Si averte quando che trovarete la chiave di G Sol re ut lasciate sonar un violino & doppo entrarete quando vi trovarete la nuova chiave C sol fa ut" (Note that when you find the clef G sol re ut [G2] you must let the violin play and then enter when you find the new clef C sol fa ut [C1]; 1618d).

49   See Table 8 for the shelf numbers of Estense manuscripts mentioned here.

50   The original print has only one bass partbook, labelled *organo*, but the continuo bass in that volume is more active than usual in church sonatas, so that it is not surprising to find active melodic bass parts in the manuscript source. Why they were not transmitted in the print is a mystery.

51   On the transition from violone to violoncello, see Stephen Bonta, "From Violone to Violoncello: A Question of Strings?" *Journal of the American Musical Instrument Society* 3 (1977): 64–99; and more generally, "Terminology for the Bass Violin in Seventeenth-Century Italy," *Journal of the American Musical Instrument Society* 4 (1978): 5–43.

52   See John G. Suess, "Giovanni Battista Vitali and the 'Sonata da Chiesa'" (Ph.D. diss., Yale University, 1963); and William Klenz, *Giovanni Maria Bononcini of Modena, a Chapter in Baroque Instrumental Music* (Durham N.C.: Duke University Press, 1962).

d   The Estense Library may hold a reprint rather than the first edition.

e   These are not identified in the library's catalogue of the collection.

53   Département de la Musique, Rés. Vm7 673. See the description and catalogue by M. Alexandra Eddy, cited above, n.44.

54   Cazzati's Op.18 is complete in the manuscript; other volumes are represented by one or more pieces (the number is indicated after the date of publication). There is one further concordance to Vitali not noted by Eddy: Rost 118 is the first sonata from Vitali's Op.2.

55   N. N. Romano is actually Lelio Colista, according to Eleanor McCrickard, "Roman Repertory, " 573, n.12.

56   Most of these are newly identified, and unattributed in the manuscripts. Of the concordances listed, Eddy had already identified Cazzati's sonata and capriccio in Ms.Mus.Sch.c.80, and 3 sonatas from Vitali's Op. 2 in Ms.Mus.Sch.d.257 in her cat-alogue of the Rost manuscript; the sonatas and correnti from Legrenzi's Op.4 found in Ms.Mus.Sch.d.249 are identified in the revised description of manuscript sources by P. Ward Jones, music librarian at the Bodleian (unpublished typescript available in the library). The earlier catalogue is that of Falconer Madan, *Summary Catalogue of Western Manuscripts in the Bodleian Library*, vol. 5 (Oxford: Clarendon, 1905).

57   For example, that attributed to Colista and Stradella in several British sources.

58   For this study I have searched rigorously only for sonatas found in Italian prints pub-lished before 1675. Dances and later sonatas have come to my attention only haphaz-ardly.

59   On the availability of prints from Gardano/Magni before mid-century from one London bookseller, see D. W. Krummel, "Venetian Baroque Music in a London Bookshop," in *Music and Bibliography: Essays in Honour of Alec Hyatt King*, ed. O. Neighbor (London: K.G. Saur, Clive Bingley 1980), 1–27.

60   See note 30 above. I am indebted to Brian Crosby for corrections of my initial attempt to describe these collections; these remarks are drawn from his introduction in the *Catalogue*, xviii–xxvi.

61   Falle was ordained in 1679, Finch in 1700; John Sharp I served as chaplain to Sir Hineague Finch, the first Earl of Nottingham, then archbishop of York.

62   Durham Cathedral Library, Ms.Bamburgh M70. The original sonatas are on Reverse pp. 12–51 and 56–59, and the revisions, on Rev. pp. 66–75.

63   *Sonate a tré doi violini, e violone, col basso per l'organo di Giacomo Sherard Filarmonico*, Opera Prima (Amsterdam: Estienne Roger, 1701). On James Sherard, see Michael Tilmouth, "James Sherard: an English Amateur Composer," *Music & Letters* 47 (1966): 313–22. For further examples of the effect of travel on dissemination of and attitudes toward Italian music see Michael Tilmouth, "Music and British Travellers Abroad, 1630–1730" in *Source Materials and the Interpretation of Music*, ed. Ian Bent (London: Stainer & Bell, 1981), 357–82.

64   Erik Kjellberg, *Kungliga Musiker i Sverige under Stormaktstiden: Studier kring deras organisation, verksamheter, och status ca 1620 – ca 1720* (Institutionen för Musikvetenskap, Uppsala Universitet, 1979), 373. One of Albrici's compositions is of particular interest (Uppsala Universitetsbiblioteket, Dübensamlingen IMhs 1:1). It is a sinfonia à 6, dated 1654, for three violins; viola, basso, and viola.Basso [sic]; tiorba, organ (both figured); cembalo, spinetta (both notated a tone higher than the other parts). A sinfonia and canzona are followed by a trio for the 3 violins, solo for violin 1, improvised solos for spinetta and tiorba, a repetition of the sinfonia, solo for violin 2, improvised solo for cembalo, and a repetition of the sinfonia. The soloist in the improvised passages is provided only with the figured bass (not even transposed in the cembalo and spinetta parts). Two similar pieces are found in the collection: one anonymous (IMhs 11:25) and one attributed to Gustav Düben (IMhs 3:1), the autograph source for the latter dated 10 August 1654, after Albrici's departure. Similar improvised solos over a figured bass form a part of two sonatas by Guerrieri (1673e).

65   The only Italian printed duo and trio volume evident in Kjellberg's numerous and invaluable lists in *Kungliga Musiker* is one (not otherwise identified) of Rossi's four volumes (published 1607–23), which was owned by the Swedish Royal Chapel according to a 1626 inventory: "Tryckta musikalier och musikinstrument inköpta till den kungl. svenska hovet år 1626," Bilaga 6.1, 804. Kjellberg has also catalogued the instrumental music of the Düben collection in "Instrumentalmusiken i Dübensammlingen," unpublished typescript available in the library.

66   Jiří Sehnal, "Die Musikkappelle des Olmützer Bischof Karl Leichtenstein-Castlecorn in Kremsier," *Kirchenmusikalisches Jahrbuch* N.F. Jahrgang 51 (1967): 79–123; Ernst Hermann Meyer, "Die Bedeutung der Intrumentalmusik am fürstbischöflichen Hofe zu Olomouc (Olmütz) in Kroměříž (Kremsier)," *Die Musikforschung* 9 (1956): 388–411. The collection is housed in the Stàtni Zàmek a Zahrady, Historicko-Umelecké Fondy, Hudební Archiv, Kroměříž.

67   Thirty-eight instrumentalists are said to have played in the orchestra in 1665 (Meyer, 398). Don Smithers asserts that the court orchestra functioned with as many as thirty

instrumentalists between 1664 and 1695, in *The New Grove Dictionary of Music and Musicians*, s.v. "Kroměříž."

68   *Sonate a tre quattro cinque et sei stromenti di D Pietro Andrea Ziani* Op.7 (Venice: Sala, 1678b).

69   Balletto 4, 1, and 9 paired with Corrente 5, 1, and 3, respectively.

70   This order is found as well in a Walsh print (c.1703), a unique copy of which is held in the same library (C27); in the print ten of the same dances are attributed to Ziani. *Ziani's Aires or Sonatas in 3 Parts for Two Violins and a Thorow-Bass Containing the most refined Itallian [sic] Aire with Curious Passages to Improve a Hand and Pleasant Harmony to Delight ye Ear Being Engraven from ye Author's Manuscript which was never before Printed ye whole Carefully Corected* [sic], Opera Prima (London: Walsh and Hare [c.1703]).

71   See Eddy, *The Rost Manuscript*, Table 5, xxii.

72   See my "Ad libitum Procedures in Instrumental Duos and Trios," *Early Music* 19 (1991): 28–40.

73   See Table 8 for shelf numbers of the manuscripts cited in the following discussion. Similar reductions occur in prints: the composers Cambiagho, Frisone, Rivolta and Rognoni each had one or two canzonas included in a vocal collection (1626n), some of which had been reduced from four-part originals by Gasparo Zanetti.

74   *Arie e correnti a tre, due violini e violone* (Bologna: Monti, 1678a); three partbooks (*violino* 1 and 2, *violoncello*). In the Estense manuscript source the bass partbook is labelled *violoncino*.

75   *Bononcini's Ayers in 3 Parts...with a Through Bass for the Harpsichord* (London: Walsh & Hare, c.1701). Copies are in the British Library (d.150.2) and in Durham (C38). Note that RISM lists this with the works of Giovanni Bononcini, Giovanni Maria's son.

76   *Bononcini's Aires for two Flutes and a Bass, or two Flutes with out [sic] a Bass...with a Through Bass for the Harpsichord or Bass Violin* (London: Walsh & Hare, c.1705). Copy in the British Library (d.150.1). As in many Italian sources, "without a bass" here seems to mean without the bass violin, but with the chordal continuo bass.

77   There are three partbooks, two treble (one labelled *violino secondus*) and a bass (*Bass Organo*). The revised description in the Bodleian Library suggests that these partbooks may have been copied by James Sherard as a young man.

78   Sonata 1 in C, 2 in d, 6 in G, and 11 in D. Hans Joachim Marx lists most of the recorder arrangements and manuscripts sources for Corelli in *Die Überlieferung der Werke Arcangelo Corellis: Catalogue raisonné*: (Cologne: Arno Volk Verlag, 1980); Ms.Mus.Sch.e.405 is not mentioned by Marx.

79   Based on the revised descriptions of the manuscripts, and Madan, *A Summary Catalogue.*

80   For a thorough discussion of the nature of collections, and the inferences to be made from them, see Lenore Coral, "Music in Auctions: Dissemination as a Factor of Taste," in *Source Materials and the Interpretation of Music*, 383–401.

81   Frequent errors in the parts caused Eddy "to wonder whether they were actually used for performance." Eddy, *The Rost Manuscript*, xvi.

82   However, he is not the composer of the Walsh prints cited above as *Bononcini's Ayres*, which are taken from his father's Op.12 (1678b). See note 75.

83   *The New Grove Dictionary of Music and Musicians*, s.v. "Bononcini, (2) Giovanni."

Copyists and Publishers in Italy Between 1770 and 1830

BIANCA MARIA ANTOLINI

The distribution of Italian music in the late eighteenth and early nineteenth centuries comprised a lively mixture of the activities of copyists as well as publishers. A preliminary study of the diverse methods of music publishing in this period originating in the various Italian centers reveals a number of elements for the most part previously unknown or considered of little importance by modern commentators. I intend to give an account of the preliminary findings derived from an ongoing study, indicating some problems and some new findings.

Let me begin with a brief geographical summary of the years in question, 1770–1830. What we know about the work of publishers in the different cities is much more than can be found in Sartori's *Dizionario*.[1] In some cases what we now know makes it possible to define the special characteristics of individual publishing centers.

In the last third of the eighteenth century Venice, the city that had once been the capital of Italian book production, was the first place in which an attempt to relaunch music publishing (after a hiatus of several decades) was attempted.[2] The efforts of Marescalchi & Canobbio (1773–1775), Alessandri & Scattaglia (1776-1784), and Zatta (1783–1788) provided a continuous flow of publications; Marescalchi & Canobbio published theatrical repertoire, i.e., selections in full score, while Zatta specialized in instrumental music mostly of Viennese provenance. Their combined enterprise was however not sufficient to restore Venice to the prominent position held in previous centuries. In the last decade of the eighteenth century publishing activities were only sporadic. A few short-lived attempts to restart the tradition were made by Catterino Aglietti (1793–94), Catterino Minatelli (1794–95), and Valentino Bertoja, the last a musician, impresario, and copyist who also figures as a bookseller.

In June of 1806 Giacomo Zamboni and Giacinto Maina founded the Nuova Calcografia Musicale in order to publish vocal as well as instrumental music by subscription. They seem to have failed since we know of only three editions issued by them.[3] Zamboni, like Bertoja, is better known as a copyist for Venetian theaters.[4]

In the years that followed, Venice once more disappears from the list of publishing centers, while the demand for music is met by the regular arrival of editions from Milan, Vienna, and Germany, largely through the bookseller Giuseppe Benzon, whose activities in Venice are demonstrated in his voluminous sales catalogue of 1825 and updated by supplements up to at least 1835.

Marescalchi was subsequently the originator of publications from Naples which began in 1785. By means of a ten-year privilege guaranteeing him a monopoly, he survived until at least 1795, although he is presumed to have lasted to the end of the century.[5] The only other attempt at publishing in Naples in the late eighteenth century was undertaken in 1794 by Venanzio Salvoni in collaboration with Nicola Delia but they enjoyed little success. (Salvoni, too, was active as a copyist, in his case for Neapolitan theaters, in the years 1790-1810.)[6] Yet another beginning of little consequence was that of Patrelli who on 10 January 1812 announced the creation of a new music engraving establishment in the *Monitore delle due Sicile*. He proposed "to publish all national and foreign works, modern and old, worthy of conservation for the progress of art." In December of 1817 Patrelli tried to revive his business by two means: an agreement with the administration of the royal theaters allowing him to exploit their repertoires, and the new technique of lithography. These attempts did not bring the desired results either and his establishment closed in 1820. It was, however, exactly this type of cooperation with current theatrical production that formed the basis of Giuseppe Girard's music publishing business, which was founded in 1818 and lasted for several decades. During Girard's first decade he had some competition from bookseller/publishers such as Tramater and Settembre & Negri, but this turned out not to be serious.[7]

Florence witnessed two publishing enterprises of a certain consistency in the late eighteenth century: Ranieri del Vivo (1777–1785) and Pagni & Bardi (1795–98). These were flanked by editions printed on behalf of authors, by booksellers such as Giovanni Chiari, Antonio Barchesi, Antonio Brazzini, Anton Giuseppe and Giovacchino Pagani, etc., who also sold their products.[8] In the first fifteen years of the nineteenth century music publishing stagnated in Florence, if we exclude Piatti's isolated initiative of 1805, a collection entitled *Musica a ballo dei piu celebri autori di Parigi e Londra*.[9] Publishing started up again in 1816 with the creation of Giuseppe Lorenzi's firm, which ran into stiff competition from Giuseppe Cipriani's lithography beginning in 1820. The Miniati copyists also began engraving in 1819 while in the 1820s still more publishers joined the fray with the establishment of Lorenzo Faini and Angelo Lucherini.[10]

The most important center for music publishing in the nineteenth century, however, was Milan. After the tentative tries of Giussani at the end of the eighteenth century, there is a reawakening in the field, first with Giovanni Re (1806–1809) and then with Giovanni Ricordi beginning in 1808. Luigi Scotti and Carlo Bordoni's activities also date from this period (1813).[11] Ferdinando Artaria, who had tried to get into the music business several times beginning in 1805, did not open a real publishing house until the 1820s.[12] Luigi Bertuzzi, Francesco Lucca, and Giuseppe Antonio Carulli also emerge at this time. Among the publishers named above, Ricordi, Bordoni, Artaria, and Bertuzzi were originally copyists.

While Venice, Milan, Naples, and Florence were the most active cities, we should not forget that at the same time other cities also began publishing. In Turin there were Michele Angelo Morano in 1797–98, Felice Festa in 1806, the Reycends brothers mainly between 1808 and 1812, and Tagliabò & Magrini beginning in 1818.[13] In Rome Giulio Cesare Martorelli was active from 1809 to 1814, and Ratti & Cencetti lithographed works beginning in 1821.[14] Even some provincial centers such as Leghorn enjoyed a lively music business thanks to the emporia of Micali and Pizzotti and the establishment of Fedele Gilardi's publishing house in 1821.[15]

We still need some figures to make clear the extent of the above-described activities. Obviously numerous beginnings were made in the last years of the eighteenth century and the first fifteen of the nineteenth, but only Ricordi conducted their business on a regular and stable basis, so much so that production in this period is largely documented by hand written copies. In all of the Italian centers production became significant beginning with the early years of the Restoration: in Florence from 1816 on, in Naples from 1817, in Turin from 1818. Ricordi's production, too, increased considerably during these years. With the arrival of more new publishing houses that managed to stay in business, the 1820s brought greater activity at last.

Although this renewed activity is undoubtedly attributable to the political stability of the time, certain other factors within the field of music also played a role, most significant among them Rossini's extraordinary success.[16] One can now extract meaningful figures about the quantity of publication in the early nineteenth century by systematically examining the notices of almost all publishers in local papers. Lorenzi, for example, regularly announces his new publications in the *Gazzetta di Firenze*. On 13 July 1819 he informs the readers that he has printed 250 works, while on 24 June of the following year he declares that he has published more than 500. Thus, even in the absence of a publisher's catalogue such notices provide at least some evidence of consistent production, although represented by only a few specimens surviving in libraries.[17] Similarly, several announcements in the *Giornale del Regno delle due Sicilie* give some idea of the frequency of Girard's editions and in some cases shed light on the time elapsed between the performance of an opera and its publication. In 1826 Girard had produced 500 editions; three years later he had got as high as 1,000. As a rule Girard published operatic excerpts on the occasion of their performance in Naples but his newspaper announcements show that in some cases publication followed immediately upon the premiere even of operas not put on in Naples and thus actually preceding their Neapolitan performance. This was the case, for example, of *Il Pirata* and *La Straniera* of December 1827 and April 1829 respectively.[18]

Even for a publisher such as Ricordi about whom we have detailed information, new facts such as the dates of publication between 1808 and 1815 can be established.[19] One can compare dates of deposit of publication at the Ufficio di Censura and their effective dates of issue which were regularly advertised in the *Corriere milanese* and the *Gazzetta di Milano*. The local newspapers of the time, furthermore, often carried complete publishers' catalogues, as, for example, those of Ricordi in the 27 August 1816 issue of the *Gazzetta di Milano* or Tagliabò's on 23 May 1826 in the *Gazzetta piemontese*. These announcements are also excellent sources for studying the methods of dissemination employed by publishers around the turn of the century. In Florence at the end of the eighteenth century some composers printed at their own expense and sold single works or groups of works through booksellers. Nevertheless, the most common form of organization for selling to the public was through annual subscription to a certain number of issues per year, sometimes for a certain genre of music.

In 1786, for example, Zatta proposed such a series to distribute music for different instrumental ensembles to be issued weekly in the coming year.[20] In 1797 Morano, a bookseller in Turin, promised by subscription monthly deliveries of keyboard music and music for keyboard and voice for a year.[21] There was also a plan for a monthly guitar periodical (*Biblioteca di musica per chitarra*) set up in Milan in 1808 by Giovanni Re. In his "Prospetto di associazione", Re listed the names of composers to be published.[22] The Turin firm of the Reycend Brothers announced a *Journal de musique pour guitaxe* in 1809, that was to include music for voice and guitar as well and promised monthly issues.[23] Also in Turin, Tagliabò & Magrini announced their *Giornale d'Euterpe* for guitar and flute in monthly installments.[24] Instrumental dance music, with emphasis on pieces by Gallenberg written for the San Carlo theater, was dealt with in the "Giornale periodico di musica" entitled *Tersicore* published in 1818–19 by Girard in twice-monthly installments.[25] The *Giornale di musica vocale italiana di Ricordi e Festa* was dedicated to opera: its prospectus stated the publisher's intention to publish every twenty days (beginning in February 1808) a piece from the most successful operas of Europe. The *Giornale* did not manage to meet its scheduled appearances but survived for three years. Only three pieces came out in its fourth year, 1815-16, previously unrecorded in modern catalogues.[26] The membership drive for subscribers to an annual series begun by Girard in 1820 was linked to the repertoire of the Naples theaters, but the series never came out with any regularity.[27] Given the prevalence of this kind of repertoire in Girard's catalogue, however, it was likely that his subscriptions propped up his sales in general as it did in Rome when Ratti & Cencetti set up their subscription-list in 1821.[28] In the 20s, both Ricordi, with the *Biblioteca di musica moderna* (1820), and Cipriani in Florence, with the *Giornale di musica moderna* (1821) distributed most of their music by means of such series.

Dissemination of music at this time meant not only sales, but also rentals.[29] In various cities music, in manuscript and printed copies, vocal and instrumental, could be rented. Subscriptions of this type that already existed in France and Germany were first organized in Italy in 1808 by Ferdinando Artaria in Milan; in 1814 by Ricordi; in 1818 by Tagliabò in Turin and Martorelli in Rome; a year later by Lorenzi in Florence, and in 1821 by Moniglia in Leghorn.[30]

As I said at the beginning of this article, copyists were deeply involved in the dissemination of music between 1770 and 1830, not surprisingly, since most of the publishers listed here began as copyists, usually in theatres:[31] Marescalchi, Salvoni and Patrelli in Naples; Martorelli in Rome; Bertoja and Zamboni in Venice; Festa in Turin, and Ricordi, Bordoni and Scotti in Milan. A number of copyists had, as I said, tried their hand at printing but failed and soon went back to copying. It is safe to say that during this period business methods were the same for both. Even the appearance of manuscript prevailed in printed copies. (See Ricordi's *Giornale*, Martorelli's and Patrelli's few publications and Lorenzi's early ones.)

If music for the home was gradually passing from manuscript to print (this includes vocal scores), theatrical full scores continued to be handwritten throughout the entire nineteenth century.[32] With the growth of the operatic repertoire many copyists began to build "archivi di spartiti", libraries of scores [and parts] from which impresarios, professional and amateur, could rent sets.

Here too I will give only a few examples: in 1790 Gaetano Tibaldi, a Florentine copyist, published a list in the *Gazzetta toscana* of serious operas, farces, intermezzi, and some instrumental compositions for sale or rent.[33] In 1809 Bertoja ran a note in the *Indice de' teatrali spettacoli* cataloguing serious and comic operas available from his archives. Ricordi printed a *Catalogo degli spartiti seri e oratori, opere buffe, e farse con parti di canto e orchestra che trovansi nel magazino...* in 1819. Much of what was listed there had been purchased from Bertoja in 1813. In later catalogues of publishing houses lists of rental music become regular features. More cosmically, Fernando Artaria, addressing impresarios, writes in 1814 that "having acquired a copious selected collection of scores from old and modern works, both serious and comic, that increase daily, I am in a position to satisfy any request whatsoever... and to offer some selections for sale and rent together with their vocal and instrumental parts."[34] Artaria claimed to be able to furnish a printed list. Similar notices regarding large collections of all kinds of theatrical scores offered for rent or sale can be found in newspapers, placed there by many copyists of the time. (See, for example, Arrighi in Florence in 1790, Montaldi in Milan in 1807, Martorelli in Rome in 1810 and Miniati in Florence in 1818.[35] Virtually all Italian publishers beginning in 1816 kept an archive of theatrical scores in addition to their publications for sale aimed at music lovers.

The friction between theatrical copyists and publishers that had once existed was alleviated by the fact that almost all the publishers had begun as copyists and that from the very beginning of their activities they had agreements with theaters on the sale and distribution of operas. The study of music publishing in Italy may bring unexpected rewards together with the investigation of copyists and their dissemination of manuscripts.

Endnotes

1   Claudio Sartori, *Dizionario degli editori musicali italiani* (Florence: Olschki, 1958). A more recent state of research is examined by the present author in "L'Editoria musicale in Italia dal settecento al novecento," *Le Fonti musicali in Italia. Studi e ricerche* 3 (1989): 33–55.

2   See Bianca Maria Antolini. "Editori, copisti, commercio della musica in Italia, 1770–1800," *Studi musicali* 18 (1989): 274–301.

3   I have only seen one, the full score of a duet, "Credei dell' idol mio," from an opera by Mayr, with plate number 3 and the date October 1808. A canzoncina for voice and guitar, also by Mayr, was enclosed in a prospectus of June 1808 as an example of the firm's work.

4   See Michele Girardi and Franco Rossi, *Il Teatro la Fenice. Cronologia degli spettacoli 1792–1936* (Venice: Albrizzi Editore, 1989), 68, 75, 77, 82, 84, 86, 89, 91, 94, 96, 98, 108, 112, 114, 118, 121. Zamboni was on the staff of la Fenice as copyist or "direttore de la copisteria" during several carnival seasons between 1813 and 1834. See also Francesco Melisi, ed., *Biblioteca del Conservatorio di S. Pietro a Majella di Napoli.*

Carologo dei libretti per musica dell'Ottocento (1800–1860) (Lucca: Libreria Musicale Italiana Editrice, 1990), 11, 20, 32, 42, 114, 236, 240, 277, 304.

5   For a fairly detailed history of the firm see Richard Macnutt's entry in *Music Printing and Publishing*, ed. Donald Krummel and Stanley Sadie. The Norton/Grove Handbook of Music (New York and London Norton, 1990), 331ff.

6   Antolini, "Editori, copisti," 301–22. Francesca Seller informs me that in the Naples Archivio di Stato, fondo teatri, fascio 4 are preserved some documents regarding Salvoni's activities as copyist for the San Carlo theater in the years 1803 and 1809. Opera scores copied by Salvoni are listed in Annapia Sciolari Meluzzi and Carlo Vitali, "Una preziosa raccolta di manoscritti negli Archivi musicali della RAI di Roma. Il fondo musicale Carafa di Maddaloni," *Nuova rivista musicale italiana* (1988):231–301.

7   Rosa Cafiero and Francesca Seller, "Editoria musicale a Napoli attraverso la stampa periodica: Giornale del Regno delle due Sicilie' 1817–1860, I," *Le Fonti musicali in Italia. Studi e ricerche* 3 (1989):57–90. Antolini, "Le Edizioni rossiniane" in Mauro Bucarelli, ed., *Rossini, 1792–1992. Mostra storico-documentaria* (Perugia: Electa Editori Umbri, 1992), 362.

8   Antolini, "Editori, copisti,":322–45.

9   See the advertisement in *Gazzetta universale*, 15 January, 9 February, 25 May, 26 November 1805, 27 January 1807.

10   Lorenzi announced the opening of his Gabinetto di musica e calcografia all'insegna dell'Orfeo in the *Gazzetta di Firenze*, 17 August 1816. On 9 March 1819 Francesco and Giuseppe Miniati advertise in the same paper that they are about to open a "calcografia per musica." Their first editions, Egisto Mosell, *Marciate* for band, and a Rossini overture reduced for trio of flute, clarinet, and bassoon, are advertised a few days later. The first advertisement for Cipriani's lithography appears on 27 June 1820. The controversy between Cipriani and Lorenzi is also documented in the pages of the *Gazzetta di Firenze*. See Antolini and Annalisa Bini, *Editori e librai musicali a Roma nella prima metà dell'Ottocento* (Rome: Torre d'Orfeo, 1988), 24.

11   The violinist Giovanni Re published mostly instrumental music (for guitar, violin, pianoforte) by musicians of local reputation: Alessandro Rolla, Antonio Nava, Francesco Pollini, and Giacomo Monzino. The first advertisement of Carlo Bordoni and Luigi Scotti (*Corriere milanese*, 8 March 1813) was for excerpts from Rossini's *La Pietra del paragone* and Guglielmi's *Isola di Calipso*.

12   See Artaria's advertisements, sometimes for French, sometimes for German music, in the *Corriere milanese* of 2 December 1805, 23 February and 15 October 1807, 21 November 1808, 27 June 1811, 8 March 1813, and 29 January 1814.

13   See Mario Dell'Ara, "La Stampa musicale a Torino nei primi anni del secolo XIX," *Il Gridelino-Miscellanea di studi* 3 (1992):63–104.

14   Antolini and Bini, *Editori e librai.*

15   Antolini, "Editori, copisti":346–49 (on Micale and Pizzotti). For the beginning of Gilardi's activities see *Gazzetta di Firenze* of 11 December 1821, where Gilardi advertised twelve guitar compositions by Francesco Gragnani.

16   Antolini, "Le Edizioni rossiniane."

17   The production of printed music in Italy can be examined by means of the catalogue of the Ufficio ricerche fondi musicali (URFM) in Milan which lists copies in Italian and foreign libraries.

18   R. Cafiero and F. Seller, *Editoria musicale*, 69, 70.

19 In the Ricordi catalogue of 1857 supplied with dates by Agostina Zecca Laterza, *Il Catalogo numerico Ricordi 1857 con date e indici* I (Rome: Nuovo Istituto Editoriale Italiano, 1984), the dates of this period are missing. (Editor's note: In fact, all of it can be said to be missing, since we have never been able to purchase a copy of this catalogue. As a consequence, the plate numbers below are of use to us only if we have Ricordi editions with those numbers.) The principal source for these dates, the censor's list, begins in 1816. Ricordi announced his editions in the *Corriere milanese* of 1810, i.e., plate numbers 41–42, 47, 48, 50, 53, 55–56, 58, 66, 69, and 74. In 1811 we find 85–87, 91, and 101; in 1812 100, 105–06, 108, 109, 110, 115, 119, 121, and 123; in 1813 99, 118, 124, 127–29, 131–32, 134, 136–37, 149–52, 154, and 157; in 1814 158, 160–63, 168–69, 171–78, and 180. Moreover, in the *Gazzetta di Milano* of 13 April 1816, Ricordi ran a partial catalogue containing editions published between November 1815 and March 1816 containing plate numbers 185–87, 200, 207, 211–27, and 229–61.

20 Antolini, "Editori, copisti":294–96.

21 Dell'Ara, "Torino," 11ff.

22 *Corriere milanese*, 5 October 1808. The composers named are F. Carulli, L. Moretti, G. Monzino, L. Sommariva, A. Nava, G. Majnardi, and F. Gragnani.

23 Dell'Ara, "Torino": 83.

24 Rosy Moffa, *Storia della Regia Capella di Torino del 1775 al 1870* (Turin: Centro di studi piemontesi, 1990), 140ff.

25 Cafiero and Seller, "Editoria musicale":65ff.

26 The first announcement of the *Giornale* appeared in the *Corriere milanese* on 8 February 1808. The above-mentioned catalogue of 8 August 1816 lists the three pieces that appeared in the fourth year as Farinelli, *Ginevra degli Almieri*, the duet "Te lo chiedo per l'amore"; the same composer's "Chiarina [cavatina cantata dal Sig. Mombelli]"; and from Mayr, *La Rosa bianca e la rosa rossa*, the duetto "E deserto il bosco intorno." Imogen Fellinger mentions only the first three years of the *Giornale* in *Periodia musicalia* (Studien zur Musikgeschichte des 19. Jahrhunderts 55) (Regensburg: Bosse, 1986).

27 Cafiero and Seller, "Editoria musicale":66.

28 Antolini and Bini, *Editori e librai*.

29 For rental libraries in other countries see Hans Lenneberg, "Early Circulating Libraries and the Dissemination of Music," *Library Quarterly* 52 (1982): 122–30.

30 See *Corriere milanese*, 21 November and 14 December 1808 (Artaria) and 2 October 1814, where Ricordi announces that he has recently received a lot of instrumental music from Vienna which he offers for sale or monthly subscriptions (i.e., rental). Moffa, *Storia della Cappella Regia*, 139 (Tagliabò); Antolini and Bini, *Editori e librai* (Martorelli). In the *Gazzetta di Firenze* of 16 March 1819, Lorenzi describes his music store where he carries Italian and foreign music, vocal and especially instrumental. See 16 January 1821 for Moniglia.

31 We have little information about theater copyists and their relationship with impresarios. A map of *copisterie* attached to theatres in the nineteenth century might be compiled on the basis of surviving opera librettos. On this subject recent literature should be particularly helpful. I refer to Maria Letizia Dorsi, *I Libretti d'opera dal 1800 al 1825 nella Biblioteca del conservatorio "G. Verdi" di Milano* (Milan: Amici della Scala, 1987), and the new series published by the Libreria Musicale Italiana Editrice Lucca in collaboration with the Società Italiana di Musicologia. F. Melisi, *Biblioteca del Conservatorio di S. Pietro a Majella di Napoli, Catalogo dei libretti per musica dell' Ottocento*, 1990.

Laura Ciancio, ed., *I Libretti per musica manoscrittie a stampa del fondo Shapiro nella collezione Fanan*, 1992. Marta Columbro, ed., *La Raccolta di libretti d'opera del Teatro San Carlo di Napoli*, 1992. Maria Rosa Massa, ed., *Libretti di melodrammi e balli nella Biblioteca Palatina di Caserta*, 1992. Giuliana Gialdroni and Teresa Gialdroni, *Libretti di melodrammi e balli nel fondo Ferrajoli della Biblioteca Apostolica Vaticana*, 1994.

32   This is true of Germany as well, although in France full scores were frequently published. (Ed.)

33   See Antolini, "Editori, copisti":353ff.

34   *Corriere milanese*, 10 November 1816.

35   Antolini, "Editori, copisti":352 (Arrighi); *Corriere milanese*, 11 November 1807 (Montaldi); Antolini and Bini, *Editori e librai* (Martorelli); *Gazzetta di Firenze*, 5 May 1818 (Miniati).

The Business Affairs
of Gabriel Fauré

LISA FEURZEIG

University of Chicago

Gabriel Fauré practiced what might be called serial monogamy with his French publishers. For fifty-five years, from 1869 to 1924, he was linked with a single publisher at a time — four altogether — not counting an occasional romance with a foreigner.

This analogy is only partly facetious; it is offered to draw attention to the personal nature of the complex relation between composer and publisher. Like a marriage, that relationship involves questions of balance of power, of cooperation, of money, and of the proper raising and control of its "offspring" — the composer's works.

Although Fauré's music goes much deeper than what is usually labelled salon music, he did frequent the Paris salons, and in one respect the salon persona fits him well: he was evidently an intensely social person, acutely aware of the people around him. His letters suggest this; he uses different styles and tones, depending on the correspondent and the circumstances. The Princesse de Polignac described him evocatively:

> He had a keen sense of humor and was intensely alive to the absurdity of the pretentious; but although he was sensitive and sentimental, he was easily carried away by new affections . . . No one could resist his charm of manner, his gaiety, his tenderness, above all his utter sincerity when a new fancy took his heart and mind, as it too often did.[1]

While his romantic interests may have been volatile, the evidence shows that Fauré was a loyal friend and companion in those relations that endured, including a long-standing friendship with his beloved teacher Saint-Saëns and a strong (although not romantic) bond with his wife, Marie.

Such a man must surely have found it important to be on good personal terms with his publishers. While he may have been less free to choose publishers, or to abandon one for another, than the princess implied was the case in purely personal relationships, it seems noteworthy that as he advanced in reputation and prestige, he changed publishers twice within seven years. Apparently his view of an ideal publishing relationship was changing. He continued to raise his standards until the end of his life, from 1913 to 1924, when he seems to have found his perfect match.

This essay traces Fauré's relationships with his four principal French publishers, paying some attention also to his foreign connections. First, though, some background information on music publishing in France during this period and on Fauré's finances.

> We wish intellectual capital to be recognized as equal in value to money capital. If it is fair for a publisher to earn money because he runs certain financial risks, we wish for the composer not to be excluded from the eventual profit of his work. We seek less one-sided contracts. The total abandonment of the property of a work, without restriction, as this is now practiced in music publishing, is something which evidently must stop.[2]

These words come from a report submitted by the Union Syndicale des Compositeurs de Musique at the Congrès National du Livre in 1921. They describe the general circumstances of music publishing in France at the very end of Fauré's life. Even at that late date, the general rule was that composers sold each work for a flat fee, with no further rights to royalties on sales or performances. "[I]n those days the publisher took the whole risk of the enterprise on his own shoulders," as Jean-Michel Nectoux points out[3] — but by the same token, if a piece sold extremely well, the windfall income went entirely to the publisher.

Not having seen Fauré's publishing contracts, I cannot say exactly what terms they included.[4] Some documents hint that there may have been some compensation beyond flat fees: monthly or annual payments, or fees for performances of the opera *Pénélope*.

While most biographies imply rather vaguely that Fauré's financial circumstances were not good, they do not cite many figures. What follows is a summary of the available information, together with some facts about income and cost of living in France during this period, to help put it in context.

In considering Fauré's income from his published music, it helps to distinguish several intertwined issues. (1) Was he in poverty or discomfort? (2) Even if he was not actually poor, to what extent did his various money-making activities interfere with his composing? (3) How did his income from his published music compare with that of his publishers? (4) How did his standard of living compare with his publishers'?

In the biography of his father, Philippe Fauré-Fremiet states that when Fauré was director of the Conservatoire (beginning in 1905, when he was sixty), his yearly income amounted to 25,000 francs: 12,000 from the Conservatoire, the rest from his combined earnings as music critic for *Figaro* and his new contract with Heugel (which was worth 6000 francs a year, according to Nectoux).[5] Fauré-Fremiet writes: "He finally earns his living comfortably: 25,000 francs. Few industrialists would be content with that!"[6]

Figures for Fauré's income before and after these years are harder to come by. It is clear that his position worsened in his last years. He was afflicted with deafness, and for that reason was obliged to give up the directorship of the Conservatoire, from which he received only a small pension. "The problem was that Fauré had only been in official Government service for 24 years, and it took a considerable effort by Paul Léon, the Minister for Fine Arts, to secure him a pension at all."[7] Paul Bertrand, one of the directors of the Heugel firm, recalls an incident near the end of Fauré's life, when Fauré came to request an advance against some upcoming performances of his opera *Pénélope*. "I will never forget the figure of this old man, already marked by death, who, at the end of a long life, knew the anguish of need, almost of misery!"[8]

Beginning in 1896 Fauré was professor of composition at the Conservatoire. His student Charles Koechlin states that Fauré's income from this job was 3000 francs, which he describes as "by no means a negligible sum." At this time, Fauré's other sources of income included private lessons, his organist position at the Madeleine (which also paid 3000 francs),[9] his position as inspector of provincial conservatories, and beginning in 1903, his music criticism for *Figaro*.[10] Even at this time, though, he appears to have found his income insufficient. He wrote to his wife on 24 March 1897, "What a pity that we don't have a little more money."[11]

In *La Condition universitaire en France au XIXe siècle*, Paul Gerbod cites some figures which help to put Fauré's income in perspective. He discusses national salaries as they were standardized in 1872. These numbers show that the range of salaries among educated professionals was quite large, even for a single job. In government ministries, salaries ranged from 1400 francs for a beginning clerk to 25,000 for the director. Secondary school teachers began with salaries under 1000 francs; a few might eventually attain salaries of 10,000 francs. A justice of the peace began with 1800 francs a year and might reach an income of 8000 francs. An army colonel's salary was about 7500 francs. A bishop received 10,000 francs.[12]

These figures suggest that Fauré's financial position was reasonable or good relative to professional people of the middle classes, but low relative to manufacturers and the aristocracy, many of whom were his admirers, friends, and patrons. While he may have suffered real need after his retirement, it appears that he was sufficiently provided for during his active professional life. A more serious problem was that his concern for financial security obliged him to take several demanding jobs, and thus deprived him of the peace and quiet he needed to compose. In fact, his best composing time was usually his summer vacation, when he travelled, often to Switzerland, and spent two or three months writing. (For that reason, the costs of hotel stays should be considered as essential expenses for Fauré, above and beyond the basic needs of a family of four living in Paris.)

Finally, it seems only fair to compare Fauré's monetary situation with those of the various publishers whose decisions had so much to do with determining his position. This line of investigation makes Fauré-Fremiet's comparison with manufacturers more understandable. The Heugel family, for example, was extremely wealthy. Jean-Yves Mollier describes their position in *L'Argent et les lettres: Histoire du capitalisme d'édition 1880–1920*:

> With a personal portfolio of 900,000 francs, real estate of 400,000 francs and a business of at least 1,300,000 francs, Jacques-Léopold Heugel had done well with the money accumulated in the sale of books and scores, and he had a full personal life, frequenting the lyric theatres . . . the beaches of Normandy, and the spas of Germany.[13]

In a complex and stratified society, Fauré's family was apparently financially comfortable by the standards of many of their contemporaries, but not in comparison with numerous associates — including music publishers — and not enough so to make it possible for Fauré to compose at leisure.

1869–1879: CHOUDENS AND BREITKOPF

The Choudens firm, Fauré's first publisher, was founded by Antoine de Choudens in 1844. The acquisition of Gounod's opera *Faust* in 1859 (for 10,000 francs) assured the company's success. The firm published mostly vocal music, including operas by Gounod, Bizet, Berlioz and Offenbach.[14] Many of Fauré's early compositions were mélodies for voice and piano, so in this respect he was a good fit to the Choudens tradition. In his ten years of association with Choudens, the firm published twenty of his songs, including one, *Sylvie*, set to a text by his publisher's son Paul Choudens.

Nectoux describes Antoine Choudens as someone "whose flair for business and lack of generosity were to make him a rich man," and mentions that he often took several years to honor his contracts.[15]

In a letter to his friend Julien Koszul dating from June 1870, Fauré referred jestingly to one of Choudens's editorial decisions which appears to have annoyed him: "I shall also enclose a copy of my romance *S'il est un charmant gazon*, which is coming out soon. Choudens, who appears to be a man of considerable wit, has given it the title *Dream of Love!* Not something that would ever have occurred to me."[16]

In 1876, Fauré's older friend, the industrialist Camille Clerc, encouraged him to submit his First Violin Sonata to the German publishers Breitkopf & Härtel. In fact, Clerc himself sent them the score, together with his own substantial music order. They agreed to publish the sonata, but they were unwilling to take any financial risk, and they set their own terms. Because of its significance, I quote their letter to Clerc of 1 November 1876 quite extensively.

> Now, having studied the work, we have to tell you that, as regards the merit of the piece, we should be delighted to include it in our catalogue of publications. However, the unfortunate fact is that a publisher is not always able to follow the intentions of the moment but must weigh up whether what he is about to publish is capable of covering the costs of publication. The Sonata in question is undoubtedly a remarkable piece of work and we like it very much, but M. Fauré's name is not known in Germany and the musical market is saturated with works of this kind, though in many cases inferior to this one. We should have great difficulty in recovering our costs were we to give the composer a royalty worthy of his work, or, to put it bluntly, we cannot publish this Sonata unless M. Fauré renounces a royalty. It is not our custom to shilly-shally over the acquisition of a work, and in any other case we should prefer to give an outright refusal; but, because of your own keen interest in your friend's work, we have felt it our duty to show you the only possibility as regards publication in Germany . . .[17]

Fauré replied to Clerc: "I am delighted to accept the offer of publication without royalties in order to have the honour of appearing in the most glorious of catalogues, and I accept without misgivings since it is what Léonard thinks I should do."[18] (Hubert Léonard was a Belgian violinist and friend of the Clercs.)

Perhaps it was as a result of this encouragement from Germany that Fauré sought to publish his next chamber work, the First Piano Quartet, in France. After being refused by Choudens and Durand, he ended his connection with the Choudens firm and "concentrated his efforts on Hamelle, who agreed to publish it, but only on condition that Fauré surrendered all his rights as author, as he had done with the Violin Sonata."[19]

1879–1905: HAMELLE

The Hamelle firm was founded in 1877 by Julien Hamelle, who entered the business by acquiring the assets of the Maho firm founded in 1851. Hamelle continued the Maho tradition of publishing collections of piano music. His principal composers, aside from Fauré, included Brahms, Dvorak, d'Indy, Saint-Saëns, and Tchaikovsky. Fauré's dealings with this company were often with Julien's son Edgard Hamelle. (In what follows, I specify Julien or Edgard whenever possible. "Hamelle" without a first name refers to the company.)

The evidence suggests that the Hamelle family, in particular Julien, saw its publishing company chiefly as a business and was mostly concerned with lowering expenses and increasing income. The firm's first transaction with Fauré, in which it agreed to publish his piano quartet only if he gave up all his rights, is a case in point. Koechlin tells the story as follows: "With the hard-headedness of the peasant, 'père Hamelle' proved sharper than his fellows. . . [the] first Quartet [he] acquired without loosening his purse-strings; indeed, with no expense beyond the engraving and printing. Added to this he had obtained, gratuitously, the rights to the profitable *Berceuse*."[20]

A letter written in 1900 supports this view of Hamelle. Fauré's friend Eugene Ysaÿe was planning to conduct a performance of the *Requiem* in Brussels. Fauré wrote to Ysaÿe as follows: "The hydra Hamelle is laid low! . . . Your letter made him tremble from head to toe, and you were quite right from every point of view to write him as you did. He promised me in the first instance not to charge you anything, and he changed his mind without telling me!"[21]

In 1924, when the Hamelle company was reissuing Fauré's *Nocturnes* in a new edition annotated by Fauré's pupil Roger-Ducasse, Fauré wrote to Roger-Ducasse, complaining about the proofs. The corrections he discussed in this letter were never made.

> I pass over the appalling stinginess that is manifest from the very beginning; your Preface ought not to be made to look like a pharmaceutical advertisement, crammed disgustingly onto a single page. But there is something more serious than that, namely the page numbering of each *Nocturne* separately. The result is that your references . . . no longer tally with the present numbering. It's Edgard's job to anticipate things like that.[22]

As with Choudens, Fauré had his disagreements with Hamelle over titles for his pieces. In a letter of 24 June 1880 to Julien Hamelle, evidently a response to suggested title changes for two songs, Fauré carefully explained his reasons for preferring his own titles.[23] In that case, he prevailed; but in 1903, according to Orledge, Hamelle gave titles to the *Huit pièces brèves* (in their second printing) against Fauré's wishes.[24] Nectoux describes a similar dispute over the title of the 'cello piece which eventually appeared as *Papillon*.[25]

In the case of the *Requiem*, Hamelle's influence extended even further. "The published version in use today did not appear until 1901, by which time its intimate conception had been expanded considerably, both in terms of length and orchestration. Hamelle probably thought this would lead to more performances, and Fauré complied with his wishes."[26]

It was during this period that Fauré became involved with an English publisher, Metzler and Co. (now J. B. Cramer). In 1896 he signed a contract which gave Metzler exclusive rights to publish his compositions in Britain, its colonies, and the United States. This firm continued to publish his music until 1899, including some of the same pieces Hamelle was publishing in France. Orledge states that "Metzler's unbusinesslike methods led to a running battle with Hamelle and their contract was not renewed in 1901."[27] In 1920, Edgard Hamelle evidently asked Fauré for some information regarding these transactions. In Fauré's reply he mentioned that he had received monthly payments of 250 francs from Metzler in 1895 or 1896 (Nectoux points out that it must have been 1896), but that the payments ended after that year.[28]

A good deal of information is available about Hamelle's payments to Fauré. In his first contract with Fauré, which included the publication without royalties of the Piano Quartet, the *Berceuse* for violin and piano and the three songs of Opus 18 are purchased for 50 francs apiece.[29] According to Koechlin, 50 francs was Hamelle's average payment for each of Fauré's songs.[30]

In August 1898, Fauré requested 700 francs for three pieces: the seventh *Nocturne*, the *Sicilienne* for 'cello and piano, and the *Fantasy* for flute.

In the same letter, he mentioned the second half of the previous year's account, 2500 francs, and politely requested that this be settled on December 1. The tone of this letter is ingratiating, as though Fauré feared that he might not get his money at all. Whether the account he referred to represented some kind of regular payment arrangement between him and Hamelle or simply the total he happened to be owed in 1897 cannot be determined from this letter. (In any case, if Hamelle had not paid this account eight months into the following year, and Fauré did not expect it before December, that suggests that Hamelle could be just as unbusinesslike as Metzler.) Four years later, in August 1902, Fauré requested 600 francs for four of the pieces eventually published as the *Huit pièces brèves* (adding that he had another piece "buzzing round in my head" which he would throw in if he could "manage to bring it off").[31]

These figures suggest that Fauré set his own prices for the pieces he offered Hamelle — although it seems likely that some negotiation occurred before the final price was reached — and that he expected to be paid approximately 200 francs per instrumental composition, probably depending on its length, salability, and so on.

We have some evidence of how the publication of a larger composition was handled from the information about Fauré's theatrical work *Prométhée*, which was composed in 1900 and performed with great success in the Arène de Béziers in the summers of 1900 and 1901. Fauré apparently hoped to have this work published by a different French publisher, Justin Robert from Béziers. He wrote to a friend in February 1900:

> On the PUBLICATION side I am truly sorry to discover that I cannot get away from Hamelle without hurting him deeply and running the risk of an extended sulk! I ought to add that he has also, for his part, made it a *sentimental* question, and all the arguments I have put up, even the demands of the poets, made no impression . . . There is, among other things, a matter of a ballet of Lalo's that Hamelle publishes, a ballet that originally flopped and that the Opéra-Comique and the Opéra *are now fighting over*; this has put him on the alert as far as matters appertaining to the theatre are concerned, whereas before he paid them little attention.[32]

Clearly Fauré took Hamelle's sentimentality with a grain of salt!

In a letter to his wife written during rehearsals for *Prométhée* before the first performance in 1900, Fauré asked if she would object if he were to request a second 500-franc advance from Hamelle. (He wanted to pay the travel expenses of his brother and niece, to make it possible for them to attend. A later letter implied that he had received the advance.)[33] Whether this money was advanced out of expected ticket receipts or sales of the score is not clear. Fauré was quite concerned with the amount of ticket receipts: in 1901 he was disappointed that they totalled only 73,000 francs, compared with 111,000 in 1900.[34] (I have not been able to determine what share of the receipts he was allotted, if any, or whether Hamelle received any of this money.)

All in all, it is clear that Fauré had good reason to be dissatisfied with the Hamelle firm, yet he remained with them from 1879 until 1905, when he signed a more advantageous contract with Heugel.[35] (It should be pointed out that he seems to have gotten on better with Edgard than with Julien Hamelle. His letters to Edgard are much less constrained, even affectionate. In 1920, according to Nectoux, Fauré approached the Minister for Education and the Arts, asking him to award Edgard Hamelle the *Légion d'honneur*.)[36] Perhaps he did not expect much from his publisher during his two and a half decades with Hamelle; perhaps he was simply biding his time, waiting for the right opportunity to come along.

In a letter to his wife written from Zurich in August 1904, Fauré wrote about a concert of French music he had attended the night before, saying:

> It made me go to bed a bit late, but I learned a lesson from this program. It is certain that commercial interest is at the bottom of everything, and if last night's program included works of Gounod and Saint-Saëns because they are illustrious, it included others, by Chabrier, Godard, Lacome and Lacombe, because the publishers of these works, instead of letting them rot in their basements, whence their native value would not suffice to bring them forth, take the trouble and risk the money to distribute them. Well, neither in this program nor in the former ones — all of which I have seen collected at the music shop of Hugo — has there been a single note from the Hamelle repertoire! And there is a concert *every evening* during the season. It is certain that [Fauré's works] *Shylock*, the *Pavane*, and *Pelléas* would fit in very well with this orchestra and the nature of these concerts.[37]

This letter suggests that the composer was reaching a turning point in his view of what services a publisher should provide. Within a year, he had left Hamelle for Heugel.

Nectoux concludes in his first summary of the relation between Fauré and Hamelle that Hamelle's "unshakable good-will" outweighed the publisher's shortcomings — especially since Fauré was not particularly ambitious.[38] Later in his biography, though, he quotes a previously un-published letter written by Fauré to Hamelle in 1896 — eight years earlier than the letter just cited — that is full of similar complaints. "I am simply unable to tolerate any longer your indifference to the fate of my compositions . . . . you treat me as though I was some student just out of school . . . . [while my colleagues' music] is circulated far and wide too, because their publishers *take trouble over them*." Nectoux guesses that Hamelle handled this protest by making promises to Fauré — and then forgetting them. He concludes that "[w]ithout painting Hamelle too black it has to be admitted that his lack of commercial dynamism and his strong mean streak hampered the popularisation of Fauré's music."[39]

The fact that such an authority on Fauré presents a rather unclear picture of Hamelle's character brings out the ambiguous nature of this relationship. Like most artists, Fauré had other things to do than promote his own work, and his annoyance with Hamelle for failing to do so apparently fluctuated. Comments in his letters suggest that his awareness of his need for a publisher's help in arranging performances was growing — and that his new view of an ideal publisher was emerging.

1905–1913: HEUGEL

For Fauré, signing a contract with Heugel & Cie was moving up to the major leagues. In several ways, this company was a more substantial and respectable member of the music world. Its founders, Jacques-Léopold Heugel and Antoine Meissonnier, who began working together in 1839, were both musically trained. The company was the publisher of *Le Ménestrel*, an influential music journal. Jacques-Léopold Heugel was active in various professional organizations, including the SACEM (Société des Auteurs, Compositeurs et Éditeurs de Musique) and a committee that worked on formulating international laws about artistic property. He worked actively on behalf of authors and publishers against copyright infringement.

When Jacques-Léopold died in 1883, the company was taken over by his son Henri. Henri Heugel increased the assets of the already successful enterprise by buying out some other significant publishers and accurately foreseeing the direction of public taste. For example, in 1882 he purchased the rights to the works of Johann Strauss for 20,000 francs. Other composers whose works were published by Heugel at this time included Offenbach, Thomas, Delibes, and Massenet. In other words, the Heugel catalog featured the popular successes of French Romantic music.[40]

Fauré's association with Heugel was favorable to him in one respect: he received significantly higher fees than he had with Hamelle. It was clouded, however, by two circumstances: the pressure on Fauré caused by the quota he agreed to in his first contract with Heugel, and the unpleasantness surrounding the printing of the parts for his opera *Pénélope*.

"The first contract between Fauré and Heugel," writes Nectoux, "dated 11 July 1905, stipulated thirty compositions to be delivered between 1 January 1906 and 1 January 1909. Fauré fairly soon realized that he would not be able to supply the number required . . . The number thirty was never reached, and this obligation was removed from the next contract."[41] Nectoux adds that this obligation led Fauré to revise old material and to write several short pieces in his effort to fulfill the contract.

Fauré's letters during this period show that his awareness of this contractual obligation troubled him and affected his decisions of what to compose. As early as 14 August 1905, just over a month after the three-year agreement was signed, he wrote to his wife:

> I am delighted to have a piece all ready for the month of January as a first move in the game with Heugel . . . It has eight beautiful pages, and I am very proud of the ease with which I completed it in three days . . . I have begun another. But I will not work on it until after the quintet.[42]

Apparently Fauré saw the contract as a challenge to learn to compose quickly. At this time, he had just been appointed director of the Conservatoire, and his time for serious composing was limited mostly to summer vacations. Long pieces, including chamber works and, of course, his opera, often took several years to complete. His decision to compose the second short piece only after doing some work on his quintet reveals his effort to balance the contract's demand for a certain number of pieces against his own need to use this vacation time for his longer, more time-consuming works.

For Fauré to mention the length of the first piece he wrote for Heugel is not an isolated instance. The following summer, he predicted Heugel's approval of two new works, citing their length.[43] The tension caused by the quota, however, seems to have been balanced by his satisfaction that Heugel kept up his part of the bargain; in the same letter, he mentioned two good engravings of recent works that Heugel had just sent.

Fauré took a respectful and deferential tone in his letters to Heugel, addressing him as "Dear Sir and friend." In his letter to Heugel on the day he sent him the two pieces mentioned above, he took pains to describe the function and potential market for the *Ave Maria* ("I think its future will lie chiefly in the fashionable classes for young ladies and girls") and described the song as "a setting of a much less obscure and much more attractive poem than *Twilight*."[44] Whether this should be interpreted as a tactic to forestall the publisher's misgivings or, more innocuously, as evidence of Fauré's courtesy and sensitivity to the publisher's natural concerns, is hard to say.

A letter of December 1908 again reveals several of these elements. Written shortly before the end of the three-year period of the first contract, it betrays Fauré's unease over his inability to meet that commitment, and his disappointment at Heugel's method of counting pieces. His natural courtesy, though, leads him to take back his objection as soon as he voices it. This letter is also a response to Heugel's offer on a contract for *Pénélope*, which appears to have been a good one. Thus, Fauré expresses both pleasure and disappointment in this carefully crafted letter.

> I shall very willingly sign the agreement you have been good enough to offer me, the terms of which seem to me — as you say — absolutely 'fair and honest.' So I shall make haste to come round and give you my signature on my imminent return to Paris, together with my thanks . . .
>
> P.S. I must admit, I thought I was a little less in arrears because, having taken the greatest possible care over the four pieces that make up the *Low Mass*. I imagined they would count as four pieces. But I can see why, given the poor sales prospects for works of religious music nowadays, you should only be counting this as one piece. The sole purpose of all this being to assure you that I did think I was a little less in arrears.[45]

In his private correspondence, Fauré's tone could be somewhat less respectful, as when he wrote to his wife in 1909: "I have begun to work a bit, but this work so far consists only of preparing some fodder for Heugel . . ."[46] The Heugel family pride is apparently easily wounded. In an introduction to a collection of letters to and from his family that was published in 1984, François Heugel mentions a letter from 1922 in which Fauré commended his former student Messager for his negative review of a Massenet opera. Fauré wrote to Messager: "Clearly the mighty House of Heugel is trying to revive scores that have rightly fallen into oblivion . . ."[47] François Heugel angrily comments on this disloyalty from "Fauré to whom Henri Heugel paid an annual fee to assure the exclusivity of his works."[48]

Because of Fauré's difficulty filling the quota in his first contract, his second contract with Heugel, which began in 1909, was differently set up. "[H]e gave up his monthly salary (500 F) and instead agreed to sell Heugel each work (600 F) as it was written, up to a maximum of ten a year."[49] By comparison, recall that eight years before he had requested 700 francs from Hamelle for three pieces.

Pénélope occupied Fauré during the summers from 1907 to 1912. The pressure was great during the final summer, because performances were scheduled at Monte Carlo and Paris in early 1913. A series of letters to his wife during this summer chronicles the difficulties with the orchestra parts.

The first reference to this situation came in his letter of July 25. "Heugel . . . writes me that he will not have the time to engrave the orchestra parts of *Pénélope*, and . . . asks me . . . who *will pay the cost of this copy*."[50] Apparently, Heugel intended at this time to have the orchestral parts copied by hand and was unwilling to bear the cost himself; his question was whether the Paris or the Monte-Carlo theater would pay. However, Fauré's letter on August 31 suggests that all parts were in fact being engraved. Discussing the orchestration, he wrote: "I must move quickly in this matter because of the very long work of engraving the orchestral score and all the instrumental parts."[51] On September 23, Fauré said that he must send off a new installment to Heugel, "for he is at my heels."[52] Finally, writing from Monte-Carlo during rehearsals in December 1912: "Heugel writes me that he will send today . . . the first act of *Pénélope*. And as the work has been rushed (it is Heugel who speaks), the parts will be full of mistakes."[53]

Fauré's association with the Heugel company had its ups and downs. Perhaps he would have remained with them longer, except for the difficulties he experienced with regard to *Pénélope*. In such a complicated and hurried situation, it is difficult to be sure who, if anyone, is to blame for the problems. In any case, these events, like the Zurich concert of 1904, may have been a catalyst encouraging Fauré to seek yet another publisher. He left Heugel as quickly as he had joined them, signing a contract with the Durand company after his second contract had expired, in 1913.

DURAND: 1913–1924

The Durand company was different from all Fauré's previous publishers in one important respect: it was run by trained musicians. The founder, Auguste Durand (who died in 1909, before Fauré's contract with the company), was an organist in the Église Saint-Vincent de Paul who had studied at the Conservatoire as a fellow student of Franck and Saint-Saëns. His son Jacques had studied composition at the Conservatoire; some of his works were published by the company.[54] Fauré respected Jacques Durand's opinion enough to solicit his advice on what to compose.

Like the Heugels, Jacques Durand took active part in professional organizations, as vice-president and then president of the Chambre syndicale des éditeurs de musique. He wrote that it was Henri Heugel who urged him to be a candidate. "Henri Heugel guided me surely in my syndical life, and his advice later helped me to enter into the post of the presidency. I will always remain grateful to him for that."[55]

Fauré had dealt with the Durand company before 1913. He offered them his first Piano Quartet in 1879. Only after they and Choudens refused it did he sign with Hamelle. Durand had published five assorted works by Fauré in the quarter-century from 1880 to 1905. An early reference to Durand (presumably Auguste) occurs in a letter Fauré wrote to his friend Marie Clerc in 1881: one of those ambiguous comments of his which may or may not have been intended ironically.

> Durand has given me some good advice regarding the *Impromptu*: He assured me that it is not by composing music like this that I will make my mark with the real public, the proper public, the buying public! Enlightened by this counsel, I locked myself in my study and composed *Les Pages de la Reine*, a Louis XIII-style dance tune.[56]

Much of the information in this section comes directly from the second volume of Jacques Durand's memoirs. Naturally, Durand presents himself in a favorable light — but the limited evidence from other sources tends to support his picture of himself. The negative evidence is especially telling: that is, I have found no indications of overt dispute or underlying tension between Fauré and the Durand firm, such as can be found in Fauré's relations with Choudens, Hamelle, and Heugel. Durand presents himself as someone who was largely concerned with his composers, their works, and their states of mind. The mere fact that he views this as a valuable quality in a music publisher may already set him apart from many others.

In his memoirs, Durand described the beginning of the company's full association with Fauré as follows.

> My father, closely linked to this master, had already had the opportunity to publish some of his works, too rarely for our taste. Some months before the war, Gabriel Fauré being free of all commit-

ment, we had the joy of being able to negotiate with him defini-
tively. I must not forget, on this subject, the friendly mediation of
Roger-Ducasse.[57]

This account does not clear up the question of why Fauré left the Heugel
firm. If there were lingering repercussions from the rushed printing of
Pénélope, Durand may have preferred not to mention that, since his rela-
tions with Heugel were so cordial. The more innocuous possibility, that
Fauré's contract simply ran out and he then received a good offer from
Durand, cannot be ruled out.

Durand's memoirs present interesting information on two subjects: the
Durand company's efforts to help their composers and promote their
composers' music, and the personal relationship between Durand and
Fauré.

Beginning in 1910, Jacques Durand organized a series of concerts of
new French music, directed by the composers. Auguste Durand originally
had the idea of creating this concert series; he planned to present chamber
music. After his death, Jacques Durand carried out the idea, but made the
concerts orchestral. The series, known as the Concerts Durand, continued
until 1914, when the war put an end to them.[58] (Presumably none of Fauré's
music was included in this series, since his orchestral music was all written
either much earlier or after 1914.) Jacques Durand was responsible for
another type of publicity: the first biography of Fauré, which was written
by his student Louis Vuillemin and published by Durand in 1914.[59]

In 1916 Durand found a way to present some of Fauré's new music.
He organized a Festival Saint-Saëns-Fauré, which consisted of a benefit
concert for the *Ligue fraternelle des enfants de France*, an organization that
helped children displaced by the war. The concert included new song
cycles by both composers: Fauré's *Le Jardin clos*, performed by Mme.
Hatto, and Saint-Saëns' *Le Cendre rouge*, performed by Plamondon, with
the composers at the piano. Durand makes an interesting observation on
the reception of these works. "I should point out that the public accorded
a warm welcome to the two great masters and their interpreters, but that
it did not seem to appreciate the first-class new works that were presented
to them in unique circumstances!"[60]

During the war, Jacques Durand committed his company to an interesting project: the publication of a new edition of the classics. He described
his reasons: a mixture of patriotism and concern for his composers. "Our
composers did not feel like composing because of the sad events of the
war. This work of revision came in the nick of time to give French composers an occupation that would help liberate the national market from

foreign enterprise."[61] Orledge describes the situation as follows. "Financial considerations compelled both Fauré and Debussy to turn their hands to editing during the war. The cutting of supplies from Germany led Durand to commission new editions of the classics." Orledge details Fauré's work — a revised edition of Schumann's piano music, and later a collaborative revision of Bach's organ works — and comments that "neither his nor Debussy's methods were what we would today call scholarly, having little recourse to original manuscripts or early editions."[62]

Durand's anecdotes about his close relationship with Fauré are heartwarming and informative. The 1913 agreement was signed when Fauré was close to 70 years old; Durand was his publisher during the last decade of Fauré's life, and he seems to have regarded Fauré with the affection and respect one might feel for a close relative. One letter from Fauré to his wife makes it clear that Durand rejoiced on Fauré's behalf even when the Durand company was not directly concerned: he notified Fauré in 1920 of an extremely successful performance of *Pénélope*, published by Heugel.[63]

The ideas for at least three of Fauré's late works came from Durand — although Durand was reluctant to influence the composer. "Fauré, since he had entered our publishing house, had always been friendly enough to ask me for directions from the point of view of what work to undertake. When I protested against any wish to influence him, he insisted so much on this subject that I decided to suggest some genres."[64]

In a letter to Durand in September 1916, Fauré described his progress on the *Fantasy* for piano and orchestra, op. 111, and thanked Durand for suggesting the work.[65] Orledge states that the idea of writing a piano trio also came from Durand.[66] Finally, Durand states that the idea of writing a string quartet — which turned out to be Fauré's last work — was his.[67]

Quite clearly, Fauré's relationship with Durand was friendly and comfortable. Durand describes his conversations with the old man. "We often spoke of Saint-Saëns, a subject which gave him great pleasure . . . then, he also spoke to me about ultra-modern art, for which he had some appreciation."[68] Durand also describes musical sessions when Fauré came to his office to play his latest works, bringing along the requisite singers or instrumentalists.[69]

Durand tells the story of Fauré's composition of the String Quartet: his feverish work, and his falling ill almost immediately when it was finished. While Fauré lay ill, he asked his sons to write to Durand telling him that the work was complete; his signing over of the work to the Durand company was his last writing, according to Durand. Whether or not this romantic story is accurate, it is undeniable that Durand felt a close bond with the composer. He concludes: "Fauré's passing affected me greatly

. . . With this great master, a whole epoch of French music ended . . . The admirable works fortunately remain for the edification of present and future generations, but, for friends, affection cannot be replaced."[70]

In the relationship between composer and publisher, each needs something from the other. At one extreme, they use each other opportunistically; at the other, they work together with mutual understanding and respect. In his work with four French publishers, Fauré moved steadily along this spectrum. At the end of his life, he was fortunate to have a publisher who counted also as a friend.

Endnotes

1   "Memoirs of the Late Princesse Edmond de Polignac." *Horizon* 68 (August 1945), quoted in Robert Orledge, *Gabriel Fauré* (London: Eulenburg Books, 1979), 15.

2   "Nous souhaiterions de faire reconnaître le droit d'accorder au capital intellectuel une valeur égale au capital argent. S'il est juste qu'un éditeur gagne de l'argent, puisqu'il court des risques financiers certains, nous voudrions que le compositeur ne soit pas exclu du profit éventuel de son oeuvre. Nous sollicitons des contrats moins léonins. L'abandon total de la propriété d'une oeuvre, sans restrictions, ainsi que cela se pratique couramment dans l'édition musicale, est une chose qui, évidemment, doit cesser." Carol-Bérard and Grovlez, quoted in René Dumesnil, *Le Monde des musiciens* (Paris: G. Crès et Cie., 1924), 219.

3   *Gabriel Fauré: A Musical Life*, trans. Roger Nichols (Cambridge: Cambridge University Press, 1991), 488.

4   Thus far, my attempts to see the contracts have been unsuccessful. A response from the company Alphonse Leduc, now representing Fauré's publishers Hamelle and Heugel, informs me that these documents are still in the private domain.

5   *A Musical Life*, 275.

6   "Il gagne enfin sa vie convenablement: 25,000 francs. Peu d'industriels s'en contenteraient!" *Gabriel Fauré* (Paris: Rieder, 1929), 69.

7   Orledge, *Fauré*, 27.

8   "Jamais je n'oublierai la figure de ce vieillard déjà marqué par la mort, qui, à la fin d'une longue vie, connaissait l'angoisse de la gêne, presque de la misère!" *Les Éditeurs de musique* (1927), 21.

9   Nectoux, *A Musical Life*, 26.

10 Charles Koechlin, *Gabriel Fauré*, trans. Leslie Orry. (London: Dennis Dobson Ltd., 1945), 9.

11 "Quel dommage que nous n'ayons pas un peu plus d'argent." Fauré, *Letters intimes,* ed. Philippe Fauré-Fremiet (Paris: Éditions Bernard Grasset), 30. I will mention here a discrepancy between Orledge and Fauré-Fremiet. Discussing the period around 1884, Orledge cites Fauré-Fremiet as saying that the Fauré family's total income was about 2000 francs (p 13). In Fauré-Fremiet's biography, he writes that Mme. Fauré's painted

fans brought in 2000 francs per year at this time — thus, the total income must have been greater than that (p. 45). Orledge seems to have misunderstood the situation.

12   (Paris: Presses Universitaires de France, 1965), 587.

13   "Avec un portefeuille mobilier personnel de 900 000 F, des placements immobiliers de 400 000 F et une entreprise d'au moins 1 300 000 F, [Jacques-Léopold] Heugel avait très équitablement réparti l'argent accumulé dans le commerce des livres et des partitions, et il eut une vie personnelle très remplie, hantant les foyers des théâtres lyriques . . . les plages normandes et les villes d'eaux allemandes . . ." (Librairie Arthème Fayard, 1988), 350.

14   Anik Devriès and François Lesure, *Dictionnaire des éditeurs de musique français*, 2 vols. (Geneva: Minkoff, 1988), 2: 107–8.

15   Nectoux, *A Musical Life*, 22.

16   Jean-Michel Nectoux (ed.), *Gabriel Fauré: His Life through his Letters*, trans. J.A. Underwood (London: Marion Boyars, 1984), 25. In defense of Choudens, the phrase "rêve d'amour" does appear in the poem.

17   Ibid., 41.

18   Ibid., 42.

19   Orledge, *Fauré*, 66.

20   Koechlin, *Fauré*, 4–5.

21   Nectoux, *Letters*, 248–49.

22   Ibid., 336.

23   Ibid., 97.

24   Orledge, *Fauré*, 97.

25   Nectoux, *A Musical Life*, 89.

26   Orledge, *Fauré*, 110.

27   Ibid., 16.

28   Nectoux, *Letters*, 308–9.

29   Nectoux, *A Musical Life*, 85–86.

30   Koechlin, *Fauré*, 4–5.

31   Nectoux, *Letters*, 250–51.

32   Ibid., 240.

33   Fauré, *Lettres intimes*, 43 & 52.

34   Ibid., 62.

35   This contract is described as "assez avantageux" (rather advantageous) by his son Philippe in *Lettres intimes*, 108.

36   Nectoux, *Letters*, 309 note 5.

37   "Cela m'a fait coucher un peu tard, mais j'ai tiré de ce programme un enseignement. Il est bien certain que l'intérêt commercial est au fond de tout, et que si le programme d'hier comportait des oeuvres de Gounod et de Saint-Saëns parce que ces oeuvres sont illustres, il en comportait d'autres de Chabrier, de Godard, de Lacome et de Lacombe, parce que les éditeurs de ces oeuvres, au lieu de les laisser pourrir dans leur caves, d'où leur valeur ne suffirait pas à les faire sortir, se donnent de la peine et risquent de l'argent pour les répandre. Or, pas plus dans ce programme que dans d'autres précédents dont j'ai eu, chez Hugo, marchand de musique, l'ensemble sous les yeux, il n'y a pas eu une note du répertoire Hamelle! Et il y a un concert *chaque soir* durant toute la saison. Il

est certain que *Shylock*, ia *Pavane*, *Pelléas* trouveraient, avec cet orchestre et la nature de ces concerts, un très judicieux placement!" *Lettres intimes*. 87–88.

38   *A Musical Life*. 86.

39   Ibid., 274.

40   Devriès and Lesure, *Dictionnaire*, 219–22.

41   Nectoux, *Letters*, 281 note 4.

42   " . . . je suis enchanté d'avoir ainsi un mocreau tout prêt pour le mois de janvier comme entrée de jeu avec Heugel . . . Il a huit belles pages, et je suis très fier de la facilité avec laquelle je l'ai conduit en trois jours . . . J'en ai un autre commencé. Mais je n'y travaillerai qu'après le *Quintette*." *Lettres intimes*, 109–10.

43   "*L'Ave Maria* à neuf pages, la mélodie cinq. Heugel sera content." Ibid., 122.

44   Nectoux, *Letters*, 263.

45   Ibid., 280–81.

46   "J'ai commencé à travailler un peu, mais ce travail ne consiste encore qu'à préparer de la pâture pour Heugel . . ." *Lettres intimes*, 177.

47   Nectoux, *Letters*, 327.

48   "Fauré a qui Henri Heugel faisait une rente annuelle pour assurer l'exclusivité de ses oeuvres." Introduction to Danièle Pistone, *Heugel et ses musiciens* (Paris: Presses Universitaires de France, 1984). This book, by the way, does not include any Fauré letters.

49   Nectoux, *A Musical Life*, 275.

50   "Heugel . . . m'écrit qu'il n'aura pas le temps de graver les parties d'orchestre de *Pénélope*, et . . . me demande . . . qui *paiera les frais de cette copie*." *Lettres intimes*, 205.

51   "Il faut que j'avance vite à cet égard à cause du travail très long de la gravure de la partition d'orchestre et de toutes les parties séparées d'instruments." Ibid., 207.

52   "car il me talonne terriblement." Ibid., 209.

53   "Heugel m'écrit qu'il enverra aujourd'hui . . . le premier acte de *Pénélope* . . . Et comme le travail à été précipite (c'est Heugel qui parle), les parties seront remplies de fautes." Ibid., 213.

54   Devriès and Lesure, *Dictionnaire*, 151–52.

55   "Henri Heugel m'a sûrement guidé dans ma vie syndicale et ses conseils m'ont aidé à aborder, par la suite, le poste . . . de la Présidence. Je lui en resterai toujours reconnaissant." Jacques Durand, *Quelques souvenirs d'un éditeur de musique*, 2 vols. (Paris: Durand, 1924–25), 2:30–31.

56   Nectoux, *Letters*, 101.

57   "Mon père, très lié avec ce maître, avait déjà eu l'occasion de publier des oeuvres de lui, trop rarement à notre gré. Quelques mois avant la guerre, Gabriel Fauré étant libre de tout engagement, nous eumes la joie de pouvoir traiter définitivement avec lui. Je ne saurai oublier, à ce sujet, l'aimable truchement de Roger-Ducasse." Durand, *Quelques souvenirs*, 2:73–74.

58   Ibid., 2:1–3.

59   Nectoux, *A Musical Life*, 427.

60   "Je dois faire remarquer que le public réserva un chaud accueil aux deux grands maîtres et à leurs interprètes, mais qu'il ne parut pas apprécier les nouveautés de premier ordre qu'on leur présentait dans des conditions uniques!" Ibid., 2:74–75.

61   "Nos compositeurs ne se sentaient pas en verve de composer à cause des événements douloureux de la guerre. Ce travail de révision venait à point pour donner aux compositeurs français une occupation tendant à libérer la marché nationale de l'emprise étrangère." Ibid., 2:65.

62   Orledge, *Fauré*, 27.

63   Fauré, *Lettres intimes*, 262.

64   "Fauré, depuis qu'il était entré dans notre maison d'édition, avait toujours l'amabilité de me demander des directives de travail au point de vue de l'oeuvre à entreprendre. Comme je me défendais de vouloir en rien l'influencer, il insistait tellement à ce sujet que je me décidais a lui suggérer quelques genres." Durand, *Quelques souvenirs*, 2:153–54.

65   Nectoux, *Letters*, 300. (Almost all of Fauré's correspondence with Jacques Durand is lost. Two of the three letters that survive are reprinted in Nectoux's collection on pages 300 and 334, and these are addressed to 'Dear friend' and 'My very dear friend'.)

66   *Fauré*, 184.

67   Durand, *Quelques souvenirs*.

68   "Nous parlions souvent de Saint-Saëns, sujet qu'il abordait avec grand plaisir . . . puis il me parlait de l'art ultra-moderne, pour lequel il avait un gout mitigé." *Quelques souvenirs*, 2:152–53.

69   A detailed list of the works played in Durand's office under these circumstances, and the performers, is found in Durand, 2:152–53.

70   "La disparition de Fauré m'affecta beaucoup . . . Avec ce grand maître, toute une époque de la musique française s'en allait . . . Les oeuvres admirable restent heureusement pour l'édification des générations présentes et futures, mais, pour les amis, l'affection ne se remplace pas!" Ibid., 155.

Index

For Product Safety Concerns and Information please contact our EU
representative GPSR@taylorandfrancis.com
Taylor & Francis Verlag GmbH, Kaufingerstraße 24, 80331 München, Germany